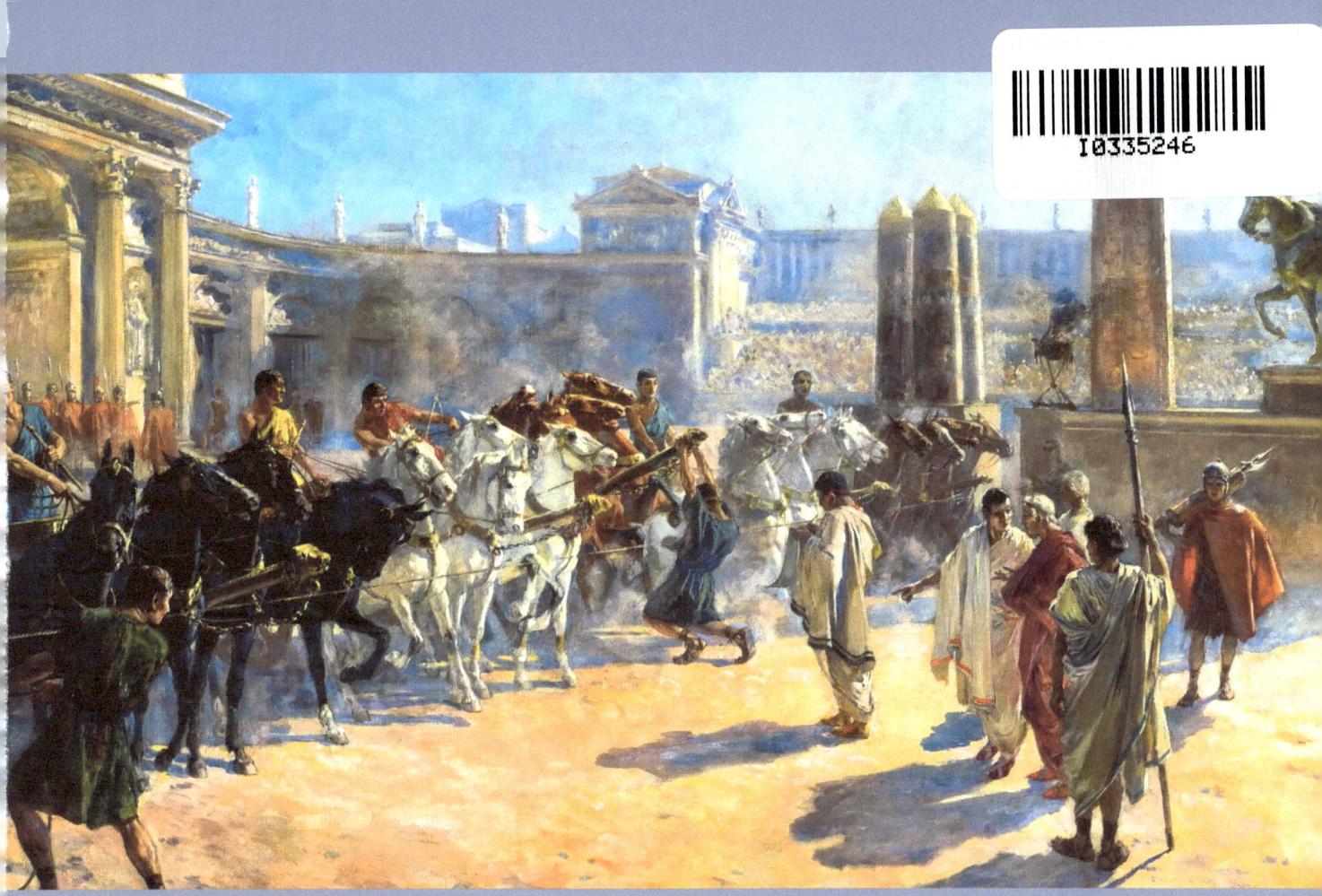

Nōn dēsistās, nōn exieris.

Don't give up, and you'll never lose.

©2022 Catherine Fet · North Landing Books · All Rights Reserved

Contents

Why Latin	1
Latin Pronunciation	2
Stress, Latin Abbreviations, **Latin Nouns: Gender**	3
Masculine Nouns	4
Feminine Nouns, Neuter Nouns	5
Island, Conversational Latin	6
Cinderella's Glass Slippers	8
Esse – To Be	9
Derive / Arrive / River	10
Latin Adjectives	11
Skirt / Shirt / Short, Names of Latin Origin	13
How Dictionaries List Latin Nouns	14
Prestige, Latin Body Parts	15
Chalk / Calcium / Calculator, Arrogance, **Nouns: Number**	17
Cherries / Peas, Nouns: Only Plural	19
Latin: The Language of Science	20
Plural Adjectives, Latin High: Consonant Gymnastics	21
Vaccine, Villain / Villa / Village, Nuclear Fusion / Fission	25
Suffixes *-ment* / *-ate*, Mercury / Merchant, 'I Have'	26
Latin Food	27
Virtue, 'I Like'	29
Latin Verbs	30
Crucial, Fame / Infant / Infantry, Stressed – Unstressed	33
Present Participles, Stance / Distance / Circumstance...	34
Crescent, Fluorescent, Incandescent...	35
Past Participles	36
Noise, Rosemary, Punishment	39
Latin High: The *Ex* Files	40
Latin Word Factories	41
Prose vs Verse	43

Latin High: Double Consonants in Past Participle Stems	44
Progress / Grade, Injury / Conjure / Perjure...	46
The 12 Most Misspelled English Words of Latin Origin	47
The Double Consonant Rule for the Last Consonant of the Root	48
Latin Cardinal Numerals	51
Onion / Union	52
Annual / Perennial / Biannual / Biennial, A Man of 3 Letters, Trivial	53
Quintessential, **Latin Ordinal Numerals**, Sequence / Prosecute / Execute...	54
Simple / Complex / Perplexed, **Latin Adjectives: Comparative Degrees**	55
Pie, *Latin Adverbs*	59
Candid / Candidate / Candle / Candy	60
Latin Landscape	61
Genitive Case	62
Accusative Case	63
2 Ways to Say 'I Have,' **Dative Case**	65
Ablative Case, 5 Cases: Endings Chart	66
Conspiracy / Inspiration, Subjugate	67
Latin Prepositions	68
Inside / Coincide, Possess / Obsess	70
Vehicle, **Latin Pronouns**	71
Ambivalent / Ambiguous / Ambidexterous	72
Suffixes *-ture* / *-able* / *-ible*	73
Admiral, Emigrant / Immigrant / Migrant, Locate / Locator...	75
Suffixes *-al* / *-ar*, Prejudice / Perpendicular / Result / Comprehend...	76
Houses and Palaces	77
Delusion / Illusion / Collusion...	78
Prefixes *de-* / *dis-*	79
Qualities of a Person	80
Homophones: Latin to the Rescue!	81
Prefer / Transfer / Differ...	83
Prefix *in-*, **Gerundive**	84
Alias / Alibi / Alien, The Longest-Possible Word Gennerator	86

Why Latin

Latin, the language of the ancient Romans, was spoken across Europe 2000 years ago. The languages of Southern Europe, such as French, Italian, and Spanish, are descendants of Latin. Although English did not come from Latin, almost 60% of its words are of Latin origin.

Latin words first appeared in the language of the Celtic inhabitants of Britain during the 367-year Roman occupation (43-410 AD). These were place names ending in
-*chester* (from the Latin *castrum* – fort),
construction and military terms, such as
mile and street (from Latin *mille* – a thousand, and *strata* - paved road).

perpendicular << pendulum

Then came the Germanic, or Anglo-Saxon invasion of Britain. Germanic tribes had waged endless wars against the Romans and had adopted lots of Latin words. They brought to Britain such words of Latin origin as
chalk, wall, wine (from Latin *calx* – limestone, *vallum* – rampart, *vinum* – wine).
After Christianity was introduced to Britain in 597, Latin spread there as the language of the church and education. Words of Latin origin that appeared in English at that time include angel, master, candle, school (from Latin ***angelus, magister, candēla, schola***).

In 1066 the Norman conquest of England flooded the English language with French words of Latin origin. Some Latin words were borrowed a second time with a different meaning! That's how we got

aviation << avīs

campus and camp (Latin *campus* – field)
candelabrum and chandelier (Latin *candelabrum* – candlestick)
cattle and capital (Medieval Latin *capitale* – property)
dominion and danger (Latin *dominus* – lord)
native and naive (Latin *nativus* – natural)
tradition and treason (Latin *trāditiō* – handing down, transfer, surrender)
price, prize and praise (Latin *pretium* – value, reward)

When book printing spread across Europe, the English language borrowed even more Latin words from classical Latin literature and works of science and philosophy.

That's how Latin became an important ingredient of English, and that's why knowing some Latin will help you improve your English spelling and grow your vocabulary.

portfolio << folium

LATIN PRONUNCIATION

There are two ways of pronouncing Latin words – **Classical Latin** – the way it was spoken in ancient Rome – and **Ecclesiastical** or **Church Latin** pronunciation that appeared in the Middle Ages. In this book we'll go with Classical pronunciation.

Reading in Latin is easy because each letter or letter combination can be pronounced only in one way. For example, in English *C* can be pronounced as 's' or 'k,' but in classical Latin it is always 'k.' In English *G* is pronounced differently in gem and in garden, but in Latin *G* is always pronounced like the 'g' in garden. Here is a list of letters and letter combinations whose pronunciation in Latin is different from their pronunciation in English.

c – as in cat
g – as in garden
a – as in father
e – as in net
i – as in machine
o – as in hot
u – as in rude

y – as *i*
ae – as in eye
au – as in mouse
eu – as e- (as in pet) + -u (as in put)
oe – as in foil
qu – as kw

feminine << fēmina

The letter *j* was not used in Classical Latin, but it appears in the medieval spelling of Latin words and is always pronounced as Latin *i* – as in machine. Let's practice reading in Latin.

structūra (structure) – strook-toora
sculptūra (sculpture) – skoolp-toora
scientia (knowledge) – skee-en-tee-a
intellegēns (intelligent) – intel-leg-ens
accidēns (accident, situation) – ak-kee-dens

discipulus (student) – dis-kee-poo-loos
saeculum (age, century) – sai-koo-loom
aureus (golden) – aa-oo-re-oos
meus (my) – me-oos

ōceanus

STRESS

In Latin, the stress falls on either the second or the third syllable from the end of the word. In the days of Ancient Rome some vowels in Latin were short and some were long. If the second syllable from the end had a long vowel, that syllable was stressed. Long vowels are marked with a sign that looks like a hyphen above the letter: ā ī ō ū

Learning to read in Latin can help you a lot with English spelling.
If you remember the Latin verb *scīre* (to know) – skee-re, you will know how to spell science, consciousness, conscience and many other English words.

Consciousness and conscience come from Latin *cōnscientia* – a joint knowledge of something.
cōnscientia << *con-* (with)+ *scīre* (to know)

address <<   ad (to) + *dīrectus* (straight)

LATIN ABBREVIATIONS USED IN THIS BOOK

e.g. = for example << *exempli gratiā* = for example
i.e. = that is, in other words << *id est* = that is
etc. = and so on << *et cetera* = and the other things
via = through, by means of << *via* = road

There are no articles in Latin!
No **A**, **AN**, or **THE**!

LATIN NOUNS - GENDER

Many English words that come directly from Latin have kept their Latin endings.
Such endings as *-us* (cactus, focus), *-a* (arena, area), *-um* (forum, album)
are the actual Latin noun endings.

Latin nouns have gender. A noun can be ***masculine, feminine,*** or **neuter**.
In English we have masculine-feminine pairs of words, like poet – poetess, waiter – waitress,
but in Latin every word has grammatical gender, including inanimate objects, e.g.
aqua (water) and *fortuna* (fortune) are feminine,
stylus (pen) and **liber** (book) are masculine,
aurum (gold) and *momentum* (motion) are neuter.

How can you tell the gender of Latin nouns? By their endings. The most common endings are:

masculine **-us**
feminine **-a**
neuter **-um**

> Neuter and neither both mean 'not either.' Only neither has an Old English root, while neuter has a Latin root.
> *neuter* << *ne-* (not) + *uter* (either of two)
> Neuter is neither masculine, nor feminine.

focus << **focus** (fireplace)

Masculine Nouns

-us is the most common ending of Latin masculine nouns.
discipulus – student, *dominus* – lord, *oceanus* – ocean, *vīrus* – poison

English words that have kept their Latin *-us* ending include:
bonus, conus, ficus, fungus, cactus, focus, census, chorus, genius, colossus, calculus, virus, consensus, apparatus, opus, stimulus

license << **licentia**

Many masculine nouns end in *-r, -er, -ir, -or* – *magister* -– teacher, *āctor* – agent

Ending *-or* was used in Latin to form nouns like *doctor* or *pastor* – people who practice this or that occupation or profession. Many English words of Latin origin have this ending:
actor, doctor, juror, dictator, orator, pastor, mentor, elector, advisor, emperor, professor, curator, animator

The English spelling rules also suggest that *-or* is used to form nouns from multi-syllable verbs that end in *-it* or *-ate*. Most of these are verbs coming directly from Latin.

absence << **absentia**

audit → auditor << ***audīre, audītum*** – to hear
credit → creditor << ***crēdere, crēditum*** – to believe
edit → editor << ***edere, editum*** – to put out, to publish
exhibit → exhibitor << ***exhibēre, exhibitum*** – to present
visit → visitor << ***vīsere, vīsum*** – to visit
accelerate → accelerator << ***accelerāre, accelerātum*** – to speed up

administrate → administrator << ***administrāre, administrātum*** – to help
animate → animator << ***animāre, animātum*** – to give life
calculate → calculator << ***calculāre, calculātum*** – to calculate

personally << persōna (mask)

The *-er* ending in English is often added to words of non-Latin origin or to words denoting objects.
lover, baker, bather, user, believer, lever, adapter, eraser, semester, computer, container
By the way, if the verb ends in vowel + consonant, the consonant will often double before *-er*
format → formatter • grab → grabber • propel → propeller • rap → rapper

Feminine Nouns

Most Latin feminine nouns end in *-a* or *-ia*

forum << forum (city square)

magistra – female teacher, ***discipula*** – female student, ***arēna*** – sand, ***area*** – open space
Feminine Latin nouns that passed into English unchanged include:
villa, idea, formula, comma, plasma, aroma, aurora, inertia, militia, area, arena, lacuna, antenna
However, most Latin words with feminine endings changed their endings in English from *-a* to *-y*.

Latin → English
familia >> family
Italia >> Italy
energīa >> energy
artēria >> artery
colōnia >> colony
anatomia >> anatomy

Ancient Romans believed that each man had a 'genius' – a spirit (similar to a guardian angel) who watched over him throughout his life. On their birthdays Roman men offered sacrifices to their genius. Later the word genius came to be associated with talent and inventiveness.
genius >> genie, ingenious, congenial

Some other, less common, feminine noun endings include *-r* and *-s*.
māter – mother • ***soror*** – sister • ***lībertās*** – freedom

Ubi lībertās, ibi patria. – Where freedom is, that's where my country shall be.
ubi...ibi... – where... there... • ***patria*** – fatherland, one's native land

Neuter Nouns

Most neuter nouns end in *-um/-ium*

minute << minūtus (small)

argentum – silver • ***monstrum*** – monster • ***mūsēum*** – museum
English words with Latin neuter ending *-um* include forum, aquarium, terrarium, minimum, maximum, stadium, podium, tantrum, premium, opium, serum, atrium, delirium, geranium

Also *-um/ium* became the standard ending for the names of chemical elements – mostly metals:
aurum, argentum, lithium, helium, calcium, aluminum, magnesium, uranium, platinum

Which chemical element gave us the word plumber? ***plumbum*** = lead
Romans had ***plumbarius*** = worker in lead. In the 19th century plumber came to mean 'the workman who installs pipes.'

Now that you know how to tell the gender of Latin nouns, see if you can sort these Latin words by gender – masculine, feminine, and neuter:
aqua – water, *terra* – land, *bellum* – war, *deus* – god, *anima* – soul, *forum* – market/square, *genius* – spirit/genius, *chorus* – chorus, *cubiculum* – room, *lingua* – language, *focus* – fireplace

ISLAND IN THE OCEANS OF SPELLING MISTAKES

Does the word island come from the Latin noun *īnsula* (island, apartment building)?
Hmmm...wait a minute... island has land in it, and land is not a Latin root.
It's a Germanic word! In Latin, land is *terra*. Land is a dead giveaway that island has nothing to do with the Latin word *īnsula*. Island comes from the Old English word *íglund* >> *iland*. At some point, however, English grammar teachers decided that *iland* was derived from *īnsula*, and demanded that an ***S*** be inserted into this word in order to make the link to *īnsula* clearer! This unforgivable mistake has given headaches to generations of students and resulted in oceans of spelling errors!

permanent << per (through) + manere (to stay)

CONVERSATIONAL LATIN

To ask in Latin 'What is this?' you would say: ***Quid est?***
Quid – what • ***est*** – is
Quid est? Liber. – What is this? A book. • ***Quid est? Stylus.*** – What is this? A pen.
Now it's your turn. Ask, ***Quid est?*** and answer using Latin words from previous pages:
What is this? Water. • A fireplace. • A square. • An ocean.

To ask 'Who is this?' you would say: ***Quis est?*** – about a man • ***Quae est?*** – about a woman.
Quae est Flavia? Flavia magistra est. – Flavia is a teacher.
Quis est Iulius? Iulius discipulus est. – Iulius is a student.

Here are a few nouns describing people:

pater – father, *māter* – mother, *soror* – sister, *frāter* – brother

>> patriot, paternal, maternal, matron, matter, material, matrix, fraternal, fraternity, sorority

The English words mother and father come from the same source as the Latin *pater* and *māter* – the Proto-Indo-European language – but they were not borrowed from Latin. Instead they arrived in English via ancient Germanic dialects.

fīlius – son, *fīlia* – daughter >> affiliate, affiliation
magister – male teacher, *magistra* – female teacher >> magistrate
discipulus – male student, *discipula* – female student >> disciple, discipline
amīcus – male friend, *amīca* – female friend >> amicable
imperātor – emperor/commander, *rēx* – king, *rēgīna* – queen,
servus – servant/slave >> regal, serve, service
fēmina – woman, *mīles* – soldier, *senātor* – senator >> feminine, female, military, militia
interpres – interpreter, *medicus* – doctor, *medica* – female doctor
Anglicus/Anglica – English man/Englishwoman, *Americānus/Americāna* – an American

Please answer the questions using these 'people' words:

Quae est Aemilia? – Aemilia is a friend. • *Quis est Flavius?* – Flavius is a teacher.
Quae est Valeria? – Valeria is a student.

To ask a question, Romans often used the suffix *-ne,* which acted as a question mark. They attached it to one of the words in the question. For example:

Estne Valeria regina? – Isn't Valeria the queen?
To answer 'yes,' you would say: *ita vērō* – so indeed
Ita vērō, Valeria regina est. – Yes, Valeria is the queen.
To answer negatively, use *nōn* – no, or *minime* – not at all
Minime, Valeria regina nōn est. – No, Valeria is not a queen.

persuade <<
per (through) + suādēre (to advise)

Let's answer a few more questions:
Estne Flavius discipulus? – No, Flavius is not a student. Flavius is a teacher.
Estne Aemilia magistra? – No, Aemilia is not a teacher. Aemilia is a doctor.

Estne Iulius mīles? – No, Iulius is not a soldier. Iulius is a senator.

Estne Augustus senātor? – No, Augustus is not a senator. Augustus is an emperor.

CINDERELLA'S GLASS SLIPPERS

Cinderella is a European fairy tale made famous in the 17th century by a French folk tales collector named Charles Perrault. There are many versions of this tale, but only Charles Perrault's version mentions a glass slipper as the item that will identify Cinderella. In other versions this item is a bracelet, a ring, or even a gold shoe. How did such a strange object as a glass slipper make its way into the *Cinderella* story? Apparently... by mistake!

Latin ***varius*** (varied) passed into French and became the source of a few French words including ***vair*** – multi-colored fur. In one of the versions of *Cinderella* the heroine had shoes (or boots) made of (or decorated with) ***vair*** – pretty multi-colored fur. That was the version Charles Perrault heard somewhere in the French countryside. Except when he heard ***vair***, he thought it was ***verre*** – 'glass' in French! Fur-trimmed boots would certainly make a much more realistic and practical gift than – ouch! – glass slippers! Charles Perrault's mistake was noticed only in the 19th century – by the great French novel writer Honoré de Balzac.

tentative << tentāre (to try)

English words coming from the Latin adjective ***varius*** and verb ***variāre, variātum*** (to vary) include:
vary, variety, variant, variation, variable, invariable

And what about Cinderella's Fairy Godmother... where does the word fairy come from? Surprise!... Fairy comes from Fate!
In Greek mythology Fates were the three dreaded goddesses of destiny spinning the threads of human lives. Sometime in the Middle Ages Fate turned into Fay – an old French word for a magical spirit of the woods, no longer a goddess. The famous sorceress Fairy Morgana, the sister of King Arthur from the legends of the *Round Table*, was called Morgan Le Fay. A mirage seen in the Straits of Messina (between Sicily and Italy) was attributed to her magical powers and became known as Fata Morgana. The magical powers of a fay were called ***faerie***. But in English ***faerie*** turned into fairy and became the word used for an individual fay – a magical spirit.

So, remember, not all fairies are fuzzy and sparkly! They are the descendants of the powerful and scary Fates! The Fates gave the English language not only fate and fairy. There is one more English word connected to the Fates. It's stamina (endurance). Latin *stāmina* means 'strings' – the threads of destiny spun by the three Fates! The longer your thread, the longer your life, the more you can endure! *Stāmina* is the plural of *stāmen* = string.

ESSE - TO BE

Quis est? – Who is this? • *Quid est?* – What is this? *Est* is a form of the Latin verb *esse* – to be. Just like the English verb to be, *esse* changes its form depending on the person – English: Singular: I am, you are, he/she/it is • Plural: we are, you are, they are

Latin *esse* – to be

I am – *sum*	we are – *sumus*	**Sic vīta est.** – Such is life.
you are – *es*	you (plural) are – *estis*	**Sine scientia ars nihil est.** –
he/she/it is – *est*	they are – *sunt*	Art (skill) without knowledge is nothing.

Romans rarely used pronouns with the verb *esse*.
I am a teacher. – ***Magister sum.*** < no pronoun I
She is a sister. – ***Soror est.*** < no pronoun she

Americanus – Americana
Britannus – Britanna

Please answer my question,
Quis es? – Who are you? (if you are a boy) • *Quae es?* – Who are you? (if you are a girl)
Use our 'people' nouns to describe yourself. For example, if you ask me, *Quae es?*
I would answer, ***Magistra sum. Māter sum. Americana sum.***

The Latin *cīvis* = citizen (plural: cīvēs) can be both, masculine and feminine.

The root of *cīvis* produced many words in English: city, citizen, civic, civilian, civility, citadel

Answer these questions in Latin:

Esne cīvis Americanus/Americana? • *Esne cīvis Britannus/Britanna?*

Esne cīvis mundī? (*mundus* = world; *cīvis mundī* = citizen of the world)

Ira furor brevis est. = Anger is a temporary (short) madness.

īra = anger >> irate • **furor** = madness >> fury, furious • *brevis* = short >> brevity

Quod est violentum, non est dūrābile. – That which is based on force/violence never lasts long.

violentus = violent >> violent, violence

dūrābilis (m., f.) *dūrābile* (n.) = lasting >> durable, durability

Usus est altera nātūra. – Habit is second nature.

ūsus = use, habit >> use, usual • *altera* = other • *nātūra* = nature

veteran <<
veterānus
(old)

Draw lines to connect English words to their Latin 'relatives':

discipline	*brevis* – short
liberal	*errō* – I err, make a mistake
liberty	*quantus* – how much?
altitude	*liber* – book
abbreviation	*dīscō* – I learn
erroneous	*altus* – high
quantity	*lībertās* – freedom

silva, rīpa, aqua, flōrēs, rīvus

A River and its Banks

Derive and arrive sound suspiciously similar. And are they both, by any chance, related to the word river? Let's investigate!

Derive means 'to get something from a source,' so it contains the idea of flowing downstream. So, yes, there is a river in derive! Actually, it's not quite a river, it's a small stream:

derive << *de-* (down from, away from) + *rīvus* (a small stream)

But arrive has nothing to do with flowing downstream. It's about arriving at a destination... maybe at a river bank? 'Bank' in Latin is *rīpa*. Arrive << *ad-* (toward) + *rīpa* (bank)

So there is a river in derive, and a bank in arrive!

Latin Adjectives

rīdiculus >>

Latin adjectives are copycats!
They copy the endings of nouns, preferring the most common ones:
-us – masculine – **bonus, malus** • **-a** – feminine – **bona, mala** • **-um** – neuter – **bonum, malum**
bonus / bona / bonum – good, kind >> bonus
malus / mala / malum – bad, evil • **malus** appears in English words as the prefix **mal-**
malnutrition = **mal-** + **nūtrire** (to nourish) = 'bad nutrition'
maleficent = **mal-** + **facere** (to do) = 'doing evil'
māgnus / māgna / māgnum – big >> magnificent, magnanimous (**magna** + **anima**=soul)
parvus / parva / parvum – small

cattus bonus – good cat • **cattus malus** – bad cat • **fabula vēra** – true story
fabula falsa – false story • **tabula rasa** – clean slate • **templum magnum** – big temple
templum parvum – small temple • **via media** – the middle path
vita beata – 'blessed life' = happiness

coordinate <<
co (with) + ōrdō (order)

What is an album? – It's something white!
albus / alba / album – white • **Album** is a singular neuter adjective.

necessārium malum – necessary evil (when you need to sacrifice something to achieve your goal)
equus Troiānus – the Trojan horse • **terra firma** – solid ground • **terra incognita** – unknown land
Rārum cārum. – Rare things are prized/expensive (Roman proverb).
rārus = rare; **rārum** = neuter singular • **cārus** = dear, expensive; **cārum** = neuter singular
Caeca invidia est. – Envy is blind. **caecus** = blind

Iūstitia caeca est.

Cum iocus est vērus,   **iocus** = joke
iocus est malus et sevērus!   **vērus** = true
When a joke is true,   **malus** = evil
that joke is evil and cruel!   **sevērus** = severe
(about people upset at the truth contained in a joke)

lībra

Abbreviation **lb** for 'pound' comes from
the Latin **libra** = balance, scales, pound of weight

If a Latin noun has an ending other than *-us, -a, um,* adjectives that describe it will still stick with the most common endings *-us, -a, um*. For example,

magister bonus – good teacher • *rara avis* – rare bird
voluntas amīca – friendliness – 'friendly will'
alma māter – 'nourishing mother' – a university from which one has graduated
magnum opus – the great work (used in English when speaking about the greatest work by an author, composer, etc.) *Opus* (work) is neuter, even though it has the *-us* ending!

Please translate word combinations below, using the following glossary:

Adjectives:
bonus, bona, bonum – good
malus, mala, malum – bad
magnus, magna, magnum – big
parvus, parva, parvum – small
verus, vera, veruum – true
falsus, falsa, falsum – untrue
novus, nova, novum – new
antiquus, antiqua, antiquum – old
sēcrētus, sēcrēta, sēcrētum – secret

Nouns:
amicus – friend
cīvis – citizen
socius – partner, ally
pictūra – picture
vīlla – country house
terra – land
vīta – life
urbs (feminine) – city
donum – gift
sīgnum – sign

Sēriōsus est!

true friend, new painting, secret sign, false friend, good citizen, old house, big land, small gift, good life, bad ally, small city, old picture, new life

Which Latin word from the list above is the source of each group of words below?
subterranean, terrace, terracotta, extraterrestrial
village, villain
civilization, civic, civil
vital, vitamin
picturesque, pictorial, pictogram, depict, pixel
signature, design, signal, designate
society, socialist, socialize
magnanimous, magnify, magnitude

Monstrum malum est!

Skirt and Shirt - You'll be shocked!

Skirt and shirt are two very different items of clothing, but the two words are suspiciously similar. They have only one letter different *k/h*. They also sound suspiciously similar to the word short...

Well, apparently there is a reason these words are so alike. They both come from the same Latin word!!! And yes, there is something 'short' in their past – a Roman tunic!
skirt, shirt << *tunica excurta* << *ex curtis* << *curtis* = short
The Roman tunic combined in itself a shirt and a skirt, and it was quite short!

Names of Latin Origin

Most Latin names came from nicknames. This explains some funny names, like
Ursula = a little she-bear << *ursa* (bear) + *-ula* (diminutive suffix).

Clara << *clāra* f. = bright • Regina << *rēgīna* = queen • Stella << *stēlla* = star
Gloria << *glōria* = glory • Leo << *leō* = lion • Felix << *fēlīx* = happy
Dominic = devoted to god << *dominus* = lord • Rosa << *rosa* = rose
Celeste = heavenly << *caelestis* << *caelum* = sky, heaven
Marina = of the sea << *marīnus* << *mare* = sea • Albina << *albus/alba/album* – white
Sabrina = from the River Severn (Severn is the longest river in Great Britain!)
Sylvia = of the forest << *silva* = forest • Victoria, Victor << *victōria* = victory
Olivia, Oliver << *olīva* = olive • Lily << Latin *lilia,* plural of *lilium* 'a lily'
Norma << *norma* = a square, a rule

Use Latin words familiar to us from these Latin names + forms of *esse* (to be) to translate the following sentences:
A star is bright. • I am happy. (*fēlīx* is both masculine and feminine)
A lily is white. • The queen is happy.
Victory is glory! • A lion is big.

column << columna

olive << olīva

How Dictionaries List Latin Nouns

Dictionaries usually give us 2 forms for each Latin noun –
the **Nominative case** form and the **Genitive case** form. What are Nominative and Genitive cases?
To show relationships between words, English uses prepositions, for example:
'the color of the rose.' Preposition <u>of</u> shows that the color belongs to the rose.
In the same situation Latin does not use a preposition. Instead, it uses the Genitive case form
of the Latin word *rosa* by changing its ending from *-a* to *-ae*.
color rosae = the color of the rose

The form changes that show relationships between the words in a phrase, are grouped into 'cases.'
The main form of the word is called the Nominative case form.
cattus – cat, *rosa* – rose are Nominative case forms.
The forms translating into English with <u>of</u> are Genitive case forms.
cattī – of the cat, belonging to the cat
rosae – of the rose, belonging to the rose

Color rosae
flāvus est.

Some Latin nouns change their stem across grammatical forms. The Genitive case form
shows whether this change happens or not. That's the reason the dictionaries always list the
Genitive case form of a noun next to its Nominative, or main, form.

Example:
tempus, n. = time
The Genitive case of *tempus* is *temporis*. *Temporis* has a different stem – not *temp*, but *tempor*.
We use *tempor* to form the plural of *tempus* – *tempora* – the times.
The Great Roman orator Cicero exclaimed in one of his famous speeches,
O tempora! O mores! – 'Oh the times! Oh the morals!'
The *tempor* stem appears in such English words as
<u>temporary, contemporaneous, contemporary, temporal</u>
If you know the two main forms of *tempus – tempus, temporis*
you'll never misspell these English words!

relevant << relevāns (helpful)

From Black Magic to Prestige

pōtiō magica

Prestige has a really crazy origin. It comes from
praestringere = to bind, to blindfold << ***pre-*** (before, in front) + ***stringere*** (to tie)
In French, *prestige* came to mean 'black magic' – the work of wizards and witches.
Prestigious was 'full of evil tricks and deception.' How did this word come to mean 'inspiring respect, having high status'? Maybe those wizards and witches were so good at what they did that their tricks became examples of excellence and prestige?

Latin Body Parts

Let's learn the names of body parts in Latin and find English words that are related to them.
For each Latin word, I will list two forms – Nominative and Genitive case, and indicate each word's gender like this:
m. – masculine, f. – feminine, n. – neuter

corpus, corporis n. – body
Many English words are related to ***corpus*** –
corpus, corps, corporal, corpuscle (a particle), corporate; corporation; corpse; corpulent; corset; incorporate.... and even leprechaun!
– from Old Irish ***luchorpan*** –
lu (little) + ***chorpan*** (body)

figūra, figūrae f. – shape, figure
>> figure, figurative, figurine
caput, capitis n. – head
>> cape, capital, capitulate, chapter, captain
faciēs, faciēī, f. – face
oculus, oculī m. – eye >> oculist, binoculars, inoculate
cor cordis n. – heart >> cordial, cardiac, cardiologist

sanguis, sanguinis, m.– blood
palma – open hand >> palm of the hand, palm tree
nāsum, nāsī n. – nose >> nasal
ōs, ōris n. – mouth >> oral
lingua, linguae, f – tongue >> linguist, linguistics
auris, auris *f.* – *ear* >> aural
digitus, digitī m. – finger >> digit (from counting on fingers!), digital, digitalize
manus, manūs, f. – hand >> manual
>>manufacture << *manus + facere, factum* (to do, to make) – 'made by hand'
>> manuscript << *manus + scrībere, scrīptum* (to write) – 'written by hand'
>> manifest << *manus + festus* (caught) – 'caught by the hand,' 'caught in the act,' indisputable
>> manicure << *manus + cūrāre, cūrātum* (to take care of)
All the words derived from *manus* are spelled with a single *N*.

latus, lateris n. – side >> lateral, equilateral (equal sides), unilateral (one-sided), bilateral (two-sided), multilateral (multi-sided), collateral (side-by-side, together), latitude
pēs, pedis m. – foot >> pedal, pedestrian, centipede, impede, expedite, expedition
cauda, caudae, f. – tail

Indicate whether the creatures on the pictures have big or small body parts:
ōs māgnum aut (or) *ōs parvum?* – a big mouth or a small mouth?
nāsum māgnum aut nāsum parvum? – a big nose or a small nose?
oculus māgnus aut oculus parvus? – a big eye or a small eye?
lingua māgna aut lingua parva? – a big tongue or a small tongue?
auris māgna aut auris parva? – a big ear or a small ear?
cauda māgna aut cauda parva? – a big tail or a small tail?

elephantus – elephant • *piscis* – fish • *crocodīlus* – crocodile • *lepus* – bunny
vulpēs – fox • *chamaeleōn* – lizard, chameleon • *serpēns* – snake

vacuum << vacuus (empty), vacuum – neuter

What's Inside Your Calculator?

There is calcium inside chalk and... inside your calculator!
The ancients used small pebbles to count and teach counting.
calx, calcis, f. – pebble, limestone
Those pebbles are still visible in chalk, calcium, and calculate.
The Latin expression **album calculum addere** – 'to give/add a white stone' refers to the ancient way of voting when casting a white stone into a voting box was equal to 'yes,' and casting a black stone was a 'no' vote.

What Do Arrogant People Want?

There is a request inside arrogance!
arrogant, arrogance << *rogāre, rogātum* = to ask, to request
So what are arrogant people asking for? They want recognition of their greatness and superiority, which are, mostly, imaginary.
Don't give them what they ask for! Tell them to go work on their attitude.

figurative << figūra (shape)

Nouns: Number - Singular and Plural

Latin nouns and adjectives can be singular or plural. While in English we use the *-s* ending to form the plural of any regular noun, in Latin the plural is different for masculine, feminine, and neuter nouns.

Masculine nouns ending in *-us, -r, -er,* and *-ir* have the ending *-ī* in plural.
digitus – digitī – fingers • *magister – magistrī* – teachers
oculus – oculī – eyes • *nūcleus – nūcleī* – little nuts

Feminine nouns ending in *-a* have the ending *-ae* in plural : *silva – silvae* – forests
figūra – figūrae – shapes • *alga – algae* – seaweed • *formula – formulae* – formulas

Neuter nouns ending in *-um* have the ending *-a* in plural: *monstrum – monstra* – monsters
strātum – strāta – blankets • *bactērium – bactēria* – bacteria

Compendia, dispendia. – Shortcuts are expensive. (Roman proverb – 'Shortcuts, losses'.)
compendia, dispendia = plural neuter nouns
compendium, compendiī, n. = shortcut • *dispendium, dispendiī,* n. = expense, loss

However, some nouns and adjectives use the *-ēs* ending to make their plural form.
māter – mātrēs – mothers • *pater – patrēs* – fathers • *frāter – frātrēs* – brothers
soror – sorōrēs – sisters • *pēs – pedēs* – feet

Quot servī, tot hostēs. – As many servants/slaves, so many enemies (Roman proverb – 'servants hate their masters').
quot...tot = as many...so • *servus, servī,* m. = slave, servant >> servile, serve, servitude, servant
hostis, hostis, m., f. = enemi, plural: *hostēs* >> hostile, hostility

Ubi opes, ibi amīcī. – Where there is wealth, there are many friends (Roman proverb).
ops, opis, f. – wealth; plural *opēs* >> opulent, opulence • *amīcus, amīcī,* m. – friend

Use forms of the Latin verb *esse* (to be) to translate a few sentences from English into Latin.
I am – *sum* • you are – *es* • he/she/it is – *est*
we are – *sumus* • you (plural) are – *estis* • they are – *sunt*
Examples:
Frātrēs sumus. – We are brothers. • *Suntne dōna?* – Are these gifts? (*dōnum* n. – gift)

Translate into Latin:
These are bacteria.(*bactērium* n.) • Are these books? (*liber – librī* m.) • We are sisters.
Are they students? (*discipulus* m.) • You are fathers. • Are you teachers? (*magistra* f.)

In English, Latin words that keep their Latin endings often keep their Latin plural forms too.
They include: bacterium – bacteria • alga – algae • larva – larvae • nucleus – nuclei

Other English words of Latin origin have shifted to *-s* for their plural ending.
aquarium – aquariums • maximum – maximums • minimum – minimums • virus – viruses

The word *vīrus* in Latin has no plural form at all.
Its meaning is 'slime, poison,' and it's an uncountable noun.

subtle << subtilis (fine)

Some words seem to be undecided about whether to keep their original Latin plural or switch to an *-s* ending. For these words, either plural form is considered to be correct:
formulas or formulae • indexes or indices • funguses or fungi • gymnasiums or gymnasia
memorandums or memoranda • moratoriums or moratoria • referendums or referenda
curriculums or curricula • syllabuses or syllabi (the subjects in a course)

The word ignoramus (an ignorant person) comes from Latin too, but it's not a Latin noun, it's a 1st person plural form of a verb: *īgnōrāmus* – 'we don't know.' So its plural is ignoramuses.

The plural of octopus is octopuses, not octopi, because the word does not come from Latin. It is of Greek origin, and its Greek plural would have been octopodes.

CHERRIES AND PEAS ARE NOT WHAT YOU THINK!

Latin *cerasum* = cherry turned into *cerise* in French. When *cerise* arrived in English after the Norman Conquest, English speakers interpreted it as a plural, cherries, and came up with a singular – cherry!
Latin *pisum* = pea arrived in Old English as *pise*. Again, it was interpreted as a plural with the *-s* ending, and a singular form – pea was created!

ONLY PLURAL

Some Latin words exist in English only as plural forms:
data << *datum* n. (Past Participle) = given;
plural – data << *dare, datum* – to give >> database, data
media << mass media (newspapers, TV, etc.)
In Latin *medium* n. = center, middle; plural: *media*

Not from Latin!
modem
<< modulator – demodulator
codec
<< coder – decoder

The idea of the media being an intermediary, an agency between the source of information and the consumers of information, emerged in the early 20th century.
English words coming from the same root are: immediate, immediacy, intermediate, mean, medial, median, mediate, mediation, mediator, mediocre, mediocrity

opera << Latin *opus* n. = work; plural neuter: *opera* = works
The word opera – 'the works' – started to be used to describe a branch of dramatic art in the 17th century.

solemn << sōlemnitās (festival, celebration)

memorabilia – objects kept or collected because of their associations with memorable people or events
In Latin *memorābilis* (adjective) = memorable; plural, neuter: *memorābilia*
In English this word was first used in the same way we use the word memoir – a written collection of memories and accounts of events worth remembering. In the early 20th century this word changed its meaning to 'a collection of objects from the past.'

regalia << *rēgālis* (adjective) = royal; plural neuter: *rēgālia*
In Latin the plural adjective *rēgālia* came to mean 'royal things,' symbols of royal power. In modern English regalia is used to describe emblems and clothing worn as a symbol of one's status or military rank. Example: military officers in full regalia (= dressed in uniform with emblems indicating their rank)

Latin - the Language of Science

In 1687 Sir Isaac Newton published his famous work *Principia*, written in Latin. The full title of the book is *Philosophiæ Naturalis Principia Mathematica* – Mathematical Principles of Natural Philosophy. In this book Newton introduced some new scientific terms he coined in Latin. Among them are *vīs centrifuga* and *vīs centripeta*.
vīs centrifuga – the centrifugal force pulling an object away from the center
vīs f. = force • *centrifuga* << *centrum* (center) + *fugere* (to run away)
The opposite of centrifugal force is centripetal force – another word coined by Newton:
vīs centripeta – centripetal force pulling an object toward the center
centripeta << *centrum* (center) + *petere* (to aim at)

Isaac Newton's manuscript written in Latin

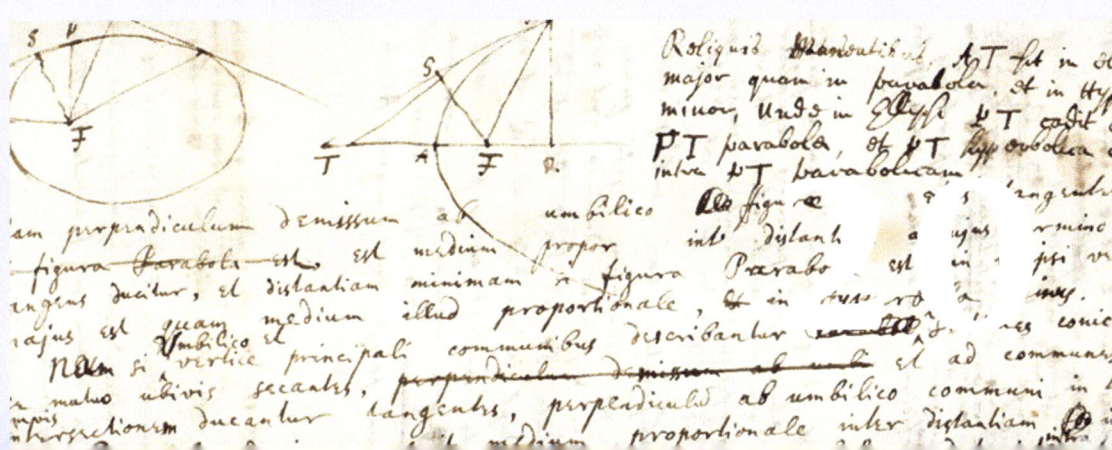

Plural Adjectives

pomegranate << grānātum

Plural adjectives mostly copycat the most common plural endings of nouns.

masculine:
bonus cattus – bonī cattī – good cats • *malus serpēns – malī serpentēs* – evil snakes

feminine:
silva māgna – silvae māgnae – big forests
terra incōgnita – terrae incōgnitae – unknown lands

neuter:
templum antīquum – templa antīqua – ancient temples
nōmen clārum – nōmena clāra – famous names

---

nomenclature
<< *nōmen* (name) + *calāre* (to call)
In Rome *nōmenclātor* was a prompter helping a politician to recall names and causes of his voters.

Difficilia, quae pulchra. – Things that are beautiful are the most difficult [to get].
'Fairest gems lie deepest.' *difficilia, pulchra* are plural neuter adjectives
difficilis = difficult; *pulcher* = beautiful • *quae* = that/which (plural, neuter)

Latin High: Consonant Gymnastics

When a Latin prefix ends in a consonant, that consonant often changes to match the first consonant of the root that follows the prefix – <u>col-lect</u>, <u>ag-gregate</u>, <u>oc-cur</u>... If you know this habit of Latin prefixes, you'll have an easier time figuring out if you need to double consonants in English words of Latin origin. Here is the true story of how that habit was formed.

One morning, at Latin High, prefix *Con* approached the verb, on whom *Con* had a serious crush. That verb was the Reading Challenge winner, *Legere Lēctum* (to read, to gather).
'Hey, *Lēctum*, want to go to the movies together?' asked *Con*, trying to sound casual.
Lēctum, however, seemed unimpressed with her attention.
He muttered 'Huh?' and kept reading his Latin textbook.
'Ahem... hey, *Lēctum*...' *Con*'s voice was shaking and virtually inaudible. She was terrified that he would simply turn around and leave. 'We could go to the cafeteria and have some vowel ice cream, you know...like, we could sit together...'
Con imagined herself sitting next to *Lēctum* in the cafeteria: *Con* + *Lēct*...conlect... Wow. Every girl in the school would be jealous. But *Lēctum*'s eyes still scanned his book.

Con panicked. 'What if he thinks I'm ugly?' That thought slashed her heart like a knife. She was one of the prettiest prefixes at Latin High, but she certainly lacked self-confidence.

Suddenly, she had an idea: 'Hold it... I know what consonant he likes best – *L*! His own name starts with *L*...' Con dashed to the mirror and quickly swapped her *N* for *L*. A moment later she was standing next to ***Lēctum*** in her new outfit, looking like... ***Col***!
'Hi, Lecti!' She was so sure she had found a way to his heart that her voice now resonated with confidence. 'Guess what's more fun than studying Latin grammar? Sitting next to me at the cafeteria and eating vowel ice cream!'
Lēctum raised his eyes from the book. 'That's cool,' he said. 'Sure! Let's go!'

Frankly, I think he would have said 'yes' right away had he noticed ***Con***, but, anyway, as they sat side-by-side, they looked like they totally belonged together: ***Col*** + ***Lēct*** = collect... which made many other girl prefixes mad with envy.

What happened next is historic. Prefixes got the idea that they could win the friendship of roots by changing their consonants to match the first consonant of the root they were trying to befriend! If you ask me, it's silly. It's a needy behavior. But many prefixes rushed to change their consonants. Hey, it worked for ***Con*** – !
In turned into ***Il*** to attract the attention of roots starting with *L*.
in- + *lēx, lēgis* (law) >> illegal • *in-* + *lūmen* (light) >> illuminate
in- + *lūstrāre, lūstrātum* (to purify, to illuminate) >> illustrate

recommend <<
re- (again) + com (with) + mandare (to take control over)

Ob (to, toward, against) went out of her way changing her consonants to match as many roots as she could!
ob- + *currere* (run) >> occur • *ob-* + *capere* (to take) >> occupy
ob- + *ponere* (to put, to set) >> oppose, opponent, opposite
ob- + *ferre* (to bring, to carry) >> offer
Prefix *ob-* is what they call 'an opportunist': It never misses an opportunity to make friends with important roots even if that means losing its identity! Speaking of opportunists,
ob- + *portus* (port, harbor) >> opportunity

Prefix ***Ad*** turned into ***Ag*** to capture the attention of the verb ***Gregārī*** (to gather), a popular gregarious kid who led the Latin High gymnastics team. I am sure you've heard of them:
ad- + *gregārī* (to gather) = aggregate

Of course, only the prefixes that end in a consonant, like **Con, In, Ob,** and **Ad** could do that consonant swapping. The prefixes that ended in a vowel, like **Pre, De,** and **Re** couldn't match the verbs' consonants. They felt left out and gossipped behind the **Ad**'s back saying she became **Ag** only to be accepted on the school gymnastics team.
That's how consonant swapping came to be known as the 'consonant gymnastics.'

Take a look at *con-* performing its consonant gymnastics:
correct = **con-** + **rect** (from Latin **regere** = to move in a straight line, to rule)
collect = **con-** + **lect** (from Latin **legere** = to read, to gather)
collapse = **con-** + **lābī /lapse** (to slide, to perish)
commit = **con-** + **mittere** (to send, to throw)
command = **con-** + **mandāre** (to commit, to entrust)
colleague = **con-** + **legere** (to read, to gather)
collaborate = **con-** + **labōrāre** (to work)

regime, regimen << regimen (control)

con- appears as *con-* before roots starting with **T, D,** because **N** is pronounced by placing your tongue behind your teeth, just like **T** and **D**. >> <u>continue, condition, contortion</u>

However, *con-* changes to *com-* before roots starting with **B** or **P**. Why? Because **M** is pronounced with your lips, just like **B** and **P**. >> <u>combination, companion, combustion</u>

ad- carries the idea of moving 'in the direction of.' *Ad-* is a real champion of 'consonant gymnastics.'
accept = **ad-** + **capere** (to take)
arrest = **ad-** + **restāre** (to stop)
affect = **ad-** + **facere** (to do)
aggregate = **ad-** + **gregārī** (to gather)
approach = **ad-** + **propiare** (to approach)
announce = **ad-** + **nuntius** (messenger)
attend = **ad-** + **tendere** (to stretch)
assist = **ad-** + **sistere** (to stop, to set) • abbreviate = **ad-** + **brevis** (short)
alliance = **ad-** + **ligare** (to tie) • attract = **ad-** + **trahere** (to pull)
affix = ad- + **fīgere, fīxum** (to fix) • assign = **ad-** + **sīgnāre** (to mark)

to <u>adlib</u> = to improvise
(e.g. 'an adlib joke,' 'an adlib speech')
adlib << *ad libitum*
<< *ad* (toward) + *libitum* (fun, pleasure)
<< *libet* (it's pleasing, it's agreeable)

Prefix **ad-** is so desperate to be friends with different roots, that it attaches itself even to non-Latin roots, such as Germanic **rang/rank** – and matches the root's first consonant:
ad- + **rang** >>> arrange

inter- = between • We find this prefix in many English words – interpret, interact, interrupt. This prefix explains why there is a silent vowel **e** in the English words interest, interesting. These words come from the Latin verb
interesse – to be between, to take part in, to be important
interesse = *inter* (between) + *esse* (to be)
Interest means 'He/she/it is important' in Latin!

If **inter-** is added to the root that begins with **r**, we get double **r**:
interrupt << **inter-** + *rumpere, ruptum* (break, tear)
It's the Latin root we find in such English words as rupture, abrupt, disrupt, corrupt.
interrogate << **inter-** + *rogāre* (to ask)
inter- turns into **intel-** in words whose root starts with **l**
intelligent and intellect come from the Latin
intellegere – to understand = *inter/intel-* + *legere* (to read/gather)
intellegō – I understand • *nōn intellegō* – I don't understand

constitution <<

cōnstitūtiō
(order, nature)

Latin prefixes that end in a vowel don't change, and therefore we don't get double consonants in the English words with these prefixes. That's why prefix has one **F**, while suffix has two!
prefix << **pre-** (in front) + *fīgere, fīxum* (to fix)
suffix << **sub-** (under, after) + *fīgere, fīxum* (to fix)

This feature is super useful in checking your English spelling. If you know Latin prefixes **pro-** and **re-** which end in vowels, you won't double **F** in refer or professor.

Latin prefixes that end in vowels include
pro- = forward • propose, professor, proclaim, produce, proceed
pre- = before • precede, prevent, predict, pretend
de- = from, not • deduce, defer, depress, deport
re- = again, back • recede, recur, respect, reduce
Also: **ante-** = before, **contra-** = against, and others.

argument <<

argūmentum
(evidence)

VACCINES AND COWS - THERE IS A CONNECTION!

Vaccine comes from the Latin *vacca* – a cow. British physician Edward Jenner (1749-1823) invented the technique of preventing smallpox by injecting people with the cowpox virus which is similar to smallpox, but much milder. Latin *vaccinus* means 'from cows.' Eventually this term was applied to all kinds of vaccines.
Remember, there is a cow in a vaccine! And that means *CC*.

DO VILLAINS LIVE IN VILLAS?

Vīlla bona!

The meaning of some Latin words has changed so much on their way into English, that you almost wonder: Is it the same word?

villain is not someone who lives in a villa or in a village, but all these words – villain, villa and village – come from the Latin *villa* = country house.
vīllānus = farm laborer >> villain
The transformation of the meaning of *vīllānus* probably began with the arrogance of the wealthy toward common workers in the fields. Then it gained an additional meaning of criminality probably due to lawlessness in less populated areas of ancient and medieval Europe.

IT'S NOT ROCKET SCIENCE!

You don't need to know nuclear physics to realize that nuclear fusion has one *S,* while nuclear fission has *SS*.

$${}^{2}_{1}H + {}^{2}_{1}H \longrightarrow {}^{3}_{2}He + {}^{1}_{0}n$$

That's because fusion comes from *fundere, fūsum* – to pour, to join
fission comes from *findere, fissum* – to split.
Just in case you forgot the difference between nuclear fusion and nuclear fission. Nuclear fusion occurs when two atoms join to form a heavier atom, like when two hydrogen atoms fuse to form an atom of helium. Fusion is 'merging together.' This reaction powers the sun.
Nuclear fission occurs when a neutron hits a larger atom, such as an atom of uranium or plutonium, and splits it into smaller ones, releasing lots of energy. Fission is 'splitting apart.' This reaction is used in nuclear power plants.
See, you can start with Latin and end up a nuclear physicist!

SUFFIXES -MENT AND -ATE

In Latin, suffix **-mentum** was added to verbs to form nouns.
document << *documentum* << *docēre* (to teach) + *-mentum*
instrument << *īnstrūmentum* << *īnstruere, īnstrūctum* = to build, to instruct + *-mentum*
pigment << **pigmentum** << *pingere* (to paint) + *-mentum*
segment << *segmentum* << *secāre* (to cut) + *-mentum*
monument << *monumentum* << *monēre* (to remind) + *-mentum*

Lots of English words have the suffix *-ment* formed from *-mentum*. In the 16th century they started using suffix *-ment* even with words of non-Latin origin, such as amazement, betterment, merriment. I've seen kids misspell *-ment* as '-mint.' Well, there may be mint in mint chocolate ice cream, but there is no mint in *-ment*, people!

-ate is another English suffix of Latin origin. It comes from the Latin suffix *-atus, -ata, -atum*. You find it in such words as certificate, accurate, considerate, corporate, delicate, desperate, fortunate, graduate, immediate, literate, separate, ultimate, desolate, moderate Remember the *E* at the end!
sēparātus >> separate • *dēspērātus* >> desperate • *corporātus* >> corporate
cōnsīderātus >> considerate • *ultimitatus* >> ultimate

Mercury - the God of Merchants

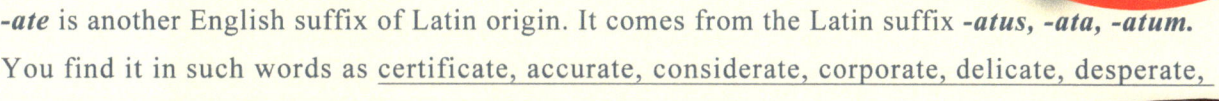

The name of the Roman god Mercury comes from **merx, mercis**, f. – merchandize Mercury was the god of traders. *Merx* also appears in
commerce, commercial, mercantile, merchant, merchandise, mercenary (a soldier for hire)

I Have

To say I have in Latin, you can say, 'Is to me...'
Est mihī stylus. – 'is to me a pen' = I have a pen. • *est* – is • *mihī* – to me
Estne tibi stylus? – 'is to you a pen?' = Do you have a pen? • *tibi* – to you

You can use the same phrase to ask about a person's name.

Quod nomen est tibi? – 'What name is to you?' = What is your name?

quod – what/which • ***nomen*** – name

Response: ***Mīhi nomen est Flavia.*** – 'to me name is Flavia' = My name is Flavia.

Please, answer in Latin: ***Quod nomen est tibi?***

Please answer using 'is to me' phrase and

ita vērō (yes) / ***minime*** (no):

Estne tibi cattus? • ***Estne tibi umbrāculum*** (umbrella)?

Estne tibi tabula subrotata (skateboard)?

Estne tibi frāter (brother) ***aut*** (or) ***soror*** (sister)?

Suntne tibi amīcī (friends)? • ***Suntne tibi librī*** (books)?

Latin Food

Napkins

One thing you need at a meal is ***mappa***... Wait, a map???
No! ***Mappa*** is Latin for napkin! Our word map of course comes from the Roman napkin! Maybe those ancient Roman navigators sketched maps on napkins while having dinner on the deck of their ship... I don't know! • napkin << Latin ***mappa*** + Middle English suffix ***-kin*** (little)

Appetite

Romans loved food and had a healthy appetite. Speaking of which...
appetite << ***ob-*** (toward) + ***petere, petītum*** (to aim at, to ask for). The Latin verb ***appetere*** means 'to desire, to crave.' The idea is, if you want something you ask for it. Other English words that came from ***petere*** = to ask include
petition, competition, competent, repetition
All these words have kept the ***pet*** root in their English spelling.

Pet is not not from Latin. It probably came from petty = little

Roman Bread

At an ancient Roman dinner they would certainly have served you ***pānis*** m. – bread
And as you and your friends are eating bread, can we call you a company?
Because company comes from ***con-*** (with) + ***panis*** (bread). Company is people who share bread! This word was coined in the 12th century in France.

All these words have the root *pan* because they have *pānis* – bread – in them:
accompaniment, accompany, companion, company, empanada, pantry
Pantry has zero connection to pots and pans: It's the room where they keep *panis* = bread!

Roman Drinks
At a meal you would certainly be offered *pōtiō*. No, it's not a magic potion, although potion
comes directly from *pōtiō* = a drink. Guess what other familiar word comes from *pōtiō*?
Poison! Good Lord! How did we go from drink to poison? Were so many drinks poisoned?

At dinner Romans drank *vīnum* = wine mixed with *aqua* = water.
As they drank, Romans said *Sānitās!* ('Health!') – the equivalent of modern Cheers!
sānitās comes from *sānus* = healthy
Interestingly, these two words went in different directions in English.
health of the body – *sānitās* << sanitation, sanitary, sanitize, sanitizer
health of the mind – *sānus* << insane, insanity, sanatorium, sane, sanity
Still, all these words have *san* – 'health' in them whether their root is stressed or unstressed.
Romans also loved milk and juice
sūcus = juice; succulent comes from *sūcus* = juice • *lāc, lactis,* n. = milk >> lactic, lactose

succulent

Favorite Roman Foods
Ancient Romans ate meat, fish, birds, eggs, fruit, vegetables, and mushrooms:
carō, carnis f. – meat << carnivorous • *piscis, piscis* m. – fish • *fungus, fungī,* m. – mushroom
avīs, avis, f. – bird << aviation, aviator, aviary – *ōvum, ōvī,* n. – egg << oval
Among Romans' favorite fruits were
mālum = an apple (spelled with a long vowel *ā* – different from *malum* = evil!)
mālum Persicum = a 'Persian apple' = a peach
mālum Armeniacum = an 'Armenian apple' = an apricot
granatum = pomegranate • *pirum* = pear • *palma, palmae,* f. = dates (from a date palm tree!)

Roman Condiments
Roman dishes were prepared with *olīvum* (olive oil), salt, and spices.
sal, salis m. – salt << saline, desalination, salami, salary, salsa, sauce, sausage
It's likely that our word salad comes from the Latin *sal* because Romans loved salt on their
vegetables. Salary comes from salarium said to be originally "salt-money" –
soldiers' allowance for purchasing salt.

condimentum = spice, seasoning

<< *condire* = to pickle fruit or vegetables in vinegar, wine, spices, etc.

Sugar was not widely available in Ancient Rome. Imported from India, it was very expensive and used only as a medicine. To sweeten their food, Romans used *mel* = honey.
English words that refer to mel include

melliloquent = able to talk sweetly << *mel + loquī, locūtum* (to speak)

mellifluent = flowing like honey

<< *mel + fluere* (to flow)

mellivorous = eating honey

<< *mel + vorāvī, vorātum* (to swallow, to devour)

There is no 'dip' in independence!
<< *in-* (inside) + *de-* (from) + *pendere* (to hang)
– 'hanging outside'!

VIRTUE

virtūs f. = manliness, qualities of a man

vir, virī, m. = man >> *virtūs* f. = manliness >> virtue

In the Roman world *virtūs* was associated with such qualities as moral character, physical fitness, courage, patriotism, and leadership. In English, it first appeared with the meaning 'life force,' 'strength,' and then became again the moral qualities of an individual – as seen in the Seven Christian Virtues – prudence (good judgment), justice, temperance (self-control), courage, faith, hope, and charity (Christian love).

I LIKE

Mālum malum est!

Use the phrase 'it pleases me': • *Lac placet mīhi.* – 'Milk pleases me' = I like milk.

placet = it pleases – singular • *placent* = they please – plural

Māla nōn placent mīhi. – 'Apples don't please me.' = I don't like apples.

māla is plural of *mālum* = apple

placet/placent are 3rd person forms of the verb *placere* = to please

English words formed from *placere* are complacent, complacency

When using this expression it is important to remember that if you like/dislike something plural – apples, cities, snakes – you should use the plural form, *placent*.

Let's take turns translating a few sentences into Latin. I'll go first:

I like oysters. (It's true! I do!) >>> ***Ostrea mihī placent.*** • ***ostreum*** n. – oyster

Your turn: I like mushrooms. >>>

fungus (plural: ***fungī***) = mushroom

> Oysters are mollusks.
> Mollusk has **LL** because
> it comes from << ***mollis*** = soft
> Another English word that comes
> from ***mollis*** is emollient (softening)

My turn: I like honey. >>> ***Mel mihī placet.***

Your turn: I like juice. >>>

sūcus = juice

My turn: I don't like bears. >> ***Ursī nōn mihī placent.***

ursus (plural: ***ursī***) = bear

Your turn: I don't like snakes. >>

serpēns (plural: ***serpēntes***) = snake

mūs

Mūs mihī placet!

serpēns

To ask 'Do you like...' use

placet + ne = placetne • ***placent + ne = placentne*** • ***tibi*** = to you

Placetne tibi aurum (gold)? – Do you like gold?
Minime, aurum mihī nōn placet. – No, I don't like gold.
Praeferō (I prefer) ***argentum*** (silver). – I prefer silver.
Placentne tibi cattī? – Do you like cats? • ***Ita vērō, cattī mihī placent.*** – Yes, I like cats.
Rīdiculī sunt. – They are funny.

> No 'dip' in department!
> department
> << ***de-*** (from) + ***partīre*** (to divide)

LATIN VERBS

We've already encountered a lot of them. Now let's learn to use them!

Infinitives of Latin verbs end in -re:

agēre = to do

audire = to hear

If you drop the -re ending, you'll get the stem of the verb:

agēre = agē + re

audire = audi + re

Latin verb stems can end in *a, e, i*.

English verbs have only 2 forms in present tense – singular and plural,
I, you, we, they – *do, work, write* • he, she, it – *does, works, writes*

Audiō et videō!

Latin verbs have 6 forms in Present Tense, for example:

ending	Present Tense form					
-ō	*amō*	I love	*videō*	I see	*audiō*	I hear
-s	*amās*	you love	*vidēs*	you see	*audīs*	you hear
-t	*amat*	he/she/it loves	*videt*	he/she/it sees	*audit*	s/he hears
-mus	*amāmus*	we love	*vidēmus*	we see	*audīmus*	we hear
-tis	*amātis*	you (plural) love	*vidētis*	you (pl.) see	*audītis*	you (pl.) hear
-nt	*amant*	they love	*vident*	they see	*audiunt*	we hear

These verb endings are the same for all verbs, however the vowels at the end of the stem are different – *a, i, e.* These vowels are still present in many English words that were derived from Latin verbs.

The stem of *amāre, amātum* (to love) ends in *ā*. It's the same *ā* we find in amateur.

The stem of *vidēre, vīsum* (to see) ends in *e*. We find *vide* from *vidēre* in such English words as evident/evidence, providence, etc.

The stem of *audīre, audītum* (to hear) ends in *ī*. The stem *audi* is part of such English words as audio, audience, auditorium, audition

The stem of *scīre, scītum* (to know) also ends in *ī*. It's the *ī* we find in science.

Nihil quod admīrārī videō. – I see nothing to admire.
nihil = nothing • *quod* = that, what

salute << *salūtāre* (to greet) << *salūs* (health)

Crēde quod habēs, et habēs! – Believe that you have it, and you have it!
crēdere, crēditum = to believe • *habēre, habitum* = to have

Fēlīx qui nihil dēbet. – Happy is he who owes nothing (who is out of debt).
fēlīx = happy • *dēbēre, dēbitum* – to owe, to be in debt

Qui nōn prōficit, dēficit. – He who doesn't accomplish anything, falls behind.
prōficere, prōfectum = to accomplish, to advance >> profit, proficiency, proficient
dēficere, dēfectum = to lack, to run short >> deficit, deficiency, defect, defective

Condemnant quod nōn intellegunt.
"They condemn because they do not understand." (Cicero)

Quod scīs, nescīs. – What you know you don't know (Don't spill your secrets, keep your own counsel). • *nescīre, nescītum* = to not know • *scīre, scītum* = to know

Otiōsus animus nescit quid velit. – The idle mind doesn't know what it wants.

ōtiōsus = idle • *animus, animī,* m. = mind, soul • *velle* = to want (*vellit* = would like)

Errare humanum est. – To make mistakes is a 'human thing' (typical of humans).

errāre – to wander, to be lost, to make mistakes

Cōgitō, ergo sum. – I think, therefore I am. • *cōgitāre, cōgitātum* = to think

Ignōrantia iuris nōn excusat. – Ignorance of the law is no excuse (legal principle).

Cum dōnant, petunt. – While they give, they ask (a Roman saying about people who give small gifts planning to ask for a big favor).

dōnāre, dōnātum = to give gifts • *petere, petītum* = to ask, to aim at

Tempus omnia revēlat. – Time reveals all.

tempus, temporis, n. = time • *revēlāre, revēlātum* = to reveal >> revelation

Honōrēs mutant mōrēs. – Honors change manners (success makes a person arrogant).

mūtāre, mūtātum = to change << to mutate, mutation, mutant

A few English nouns come from the 1st person singular – the 'I' forms of Latin verbs: audio, video, credo, veto.

videō = I see << *vidēre, vīsum* – to see
audiō = I hear << *audīre, audītum* – to hear
credō = I believe << *crēdere, crēditum* – to believe
vetō = I forbid << *vetāre, vetitum* – to forbid

Some English nouns come from the 3rd person singular – the 'he/she/it' forms of Latin verbs:

interest = he/she/it is important << *inter-* + *est* (is)

dēficit = it lacks, it's not enough
<< *dēficere, dēfectum* – to lack << *de-* (down, away) + *facere* (do, make)

exit = he/she/it leaves << *exīre, exitum* – to leave << *ex-* (out of) + *īre* (to go)

habitat = he/she/it lives << h*abitāre, habitātum* – to live

tenet (a principle, a belief) = he/she/it holds << *tenēre, tentum* – to hold

trānsit = he/she/it goes over, crosses << *trānsīre, trānsitum* – to cross over << *trans-* (across) + *īre* (to go)

A credenza (from *crēdere* = to believe) is a piece of furniture – a side table. In Renaissance Italy, poisonings were so common that a special side table appeared in dining rooms. Foods were placed on the side table and tasted by servants or bodyguards.

Ignoramus (an ignorant person) comes from the 1st person plural, 'we' form
of the verb *īgnōrāre, īgnōrātum* – to not know • *īgnōrāmus* = we don't know

Use the words below to make sentences. Example: *Cattī currunt.* – Cats run.
volāre, volātum – to fly >> volatile • *volō – volās – volat – volāmus – volātis – volant*
dormīre, dormītum – to sleep << *dormiō – dormīs – dormit – dormīmus – dormītis – dormiunt*
currere, cursum – to run << curriculum, current, currency, course
currō – curris – currit – currimus – curritis – currunt
avīs f. – bird; plural: *avēs* • *canis, canis*, m. – dog; plural: *canēs* • *cattus, cattī,* m. – cat

A bird flies. • Birds love to fly. • A cat sleeps. • Cats love to sleep.
A dog runs. • Dogs love to run.

The Crux of the Matter

Crucial (extremely important) – comes from the Latin *crux, crucis* – cross.
The idea of importance comes from crossroads – the need to choose from a few options.
The word crux also exists in English, appearing in such expressions as
'the crux of the matter,' 'the crux of the problem.'
crux = a puzzling or difficult problem or the most essential part

Do Babies Serve in the Infantry?

What do fame, infant, and infantry have in common? All come from
fārī – to talk >> *fāma* = rumor, fame >> fame
fārī >> *infans* (present participle) = one who can't talk, a baby >> infant
In the Middle Ages *īnfāns* (baby) came to mean a page, – a young boy who serves a knight.
The pages who served the knights were always on foot, not on a horse. That's how the word
infantry ('foot soldiers') emerged.

Stressed and Unstressed

Whenever the syllable is stressed, we hear its vowel very clearly. Compose and dispose
cannot be misspelled. But in composition and disposition the *pos* syllable is unstressed,

so it invites a misspell. However, if you are not sure about the vowel in an unstressed syllable, you can always try to find a related word where the syllable is stressed. Most of these tricky words come from the same Latin roots!

For composition your check word is compose, for disposition – dispose, and so on.

PRESENT PARTICIPLES

A participle is a form of a verb that behaves like an adjective.
Present Participles are formed from the Present Tense stem of the verb.
Take an Infinitive form of a verb – *agēre* (to do), drop the Infinitive ending *-re* > *agēre* = *agē* + *re,* and you have the Present Tense stem – *agē*.
To form Present Participles, add *-ns* ending (singular), *ntēs / -ntia* ending (m.,f./n. plural)
agēre = to do >> *agē-* + *-ns* >> agēns = doing, acting; plural: *agentēs* (m., f.), *agentia* (n.)

In **homo sapiēns** – 'a thinking human' – *sapiēns* is a Present Participle
of the verb *sapere* = to taste, to be wise

Many English words come from Latin Present Participles.
immigrant << *immigrāns* – moving, migrating
Present Participle of *immigrāre, immigrātum* = to move
defendant << *dēfendēns*, Present Participle of *dēfendere, dēfēnsum* = to defend
tenant << *tenēns*, Present Participle of *tenēre, tentum* – to hold

Audiēns, nōn audit. – Hearing, he doesn't hear (about a person who ignores you).
audiēns, Present Participle of *audīre, audītum* = to hear >> audience

Sapiēns nōn sum. Ignoramus sum.

STANCE AND OTHER STANDING THINGS

Stance, distance, instance, substance, circumstance – they all share a stance!
In English, stance is 'the way someone stands' or 'an attitude of a person or an organization toward something.' Stance comes from *stāns,* a Present Participle of the verb *stāre* = to stand
distance << *dis-* (apart, off) + *stāns* (standing) • instance << *in-* + *stāns* (standing)
substance << *sub-* (under) + *stāns* (standing)
circumstance << *circum* (around) + *stāns* (standing)

Aliud stāns, aliud sedēns. – One thing while standing, another thing while sitting
(a Roman proverb about people who change their opinions with no good reason).
aliud = another (n.) • *sedēns*, a Present Participle of the verb *sedēre, sessum* = to sit

THE CRESCENT MOON AND OTHER GROWING THINGS

fluorescent, incandescent, adolescent, effervescent...
Looks like these words have a reason to end in *-scent*!

Indeed, *-scent* comes from the Latin *scēns*, a Present Participle suffix related to
crēscere, crētum = to grow, to increase >> *crēscēns* = growing (Present Participle of *crēscere*)
The meaning of the suffix *scēns* is 'beginning of action,' 'growing in its quality.'
A crescent moon is a 'growing moon.'

adolescent << *adultus* (adult) + *crēscēns* (growing)
iridescent << *īris, īridis,* f. = rainbow (after Iris,
the Greek goddess of the rainbow) + *crēscēns*
incandescent << *in-* (inside) + *candere* (to shine) + *crēscēns*
opalescent << *opālus* (opal) + *crēscēns*
luminescent << *lūmen* (light) + *crēscēns*
fluorescent << *fluorum* (fluorine) + *crēscēns*
obsolescent << *obsolēscere* (to wear out) << *ob-* (away) + *solere* (to use) + *crēscēns*

opal

By the way, that *-scent* explains the difference between obsolete and obsolescent:
obsolete = outdated, out of use • obsolescent = becoming obsolete

effervescent (fizzy or happy) comes from the Latin verb *fervēre* = to boil
effervescent << *ex-* (out) + *fervēre* (to boil) + *crēscēns* (growing)
So effervescent means that something is growing so bubbly that it boils over! Today we
use effervescent to describe carbonated drinks, but Romans didn't have fizzy drinks.
For them *effervēscere* meant 'to start boiling.'

When spelling these words, remember, they all have something 'growing'
about them - the suffix *-scent*.

And what about scent (smell)? Is it also 'a growing thing'? Nah. It comes from **sentīre** = to feel. In the 17th century some smarty-pants professors decided it would look 'more Latin' if it had a *C* in it. They were impressed with ascend and descend, which come from **scandere** = to climb. In other words, adding a *C* to scent was a total fail.

Those professors were stupidescent (growing stupider and stupider).

Ha-ha, I've just made up stupidescent!!!

But *stupidus* is an actual Latin word, meaning... 'stupid.' >> stupendous, stupid, stupify

Past Participles

Just like Present Participles, Past Participles are, basically, adjectives. In English written in written text and printed in printed paper are Past Participles.
Past Participles are formed from the Past Participle stems of Latin verbs.
The Past Participle stems are often different from the Present Tense stems. For example, **agēre** = to do (Infinitive) – The Present Tense stem is **agē**.
āctum = done (Past Participle) – The Past Participle stem is **āct**.
That's why dictionaries always list both, the Present Tense and the Past Participle forms of verbs, for example: **scrībere, scrīptum** – to write >> script, Scripture
scrīptum – written – is a Past Participle of *scrībere* = to write

Like adjectives, Past Participles have gender and number:
Singular: **scrīptus** m., **scrīpta** f., **scrīptum** n. • Plural: **scrīpti** m., **scrīptae** f., **scrīpta** n.
Verba volant, scripta manent. – Words (spoken) fly away, what's written stays.
verbum, verbī, n. – word • **volāre, volātum** – to fly • **manēre, mānsum** – to remain
ācta, nōn verba = actions, not words
actum – 'done' is a Past Participle of *agere, āctum* – to act
Singular: **āctus, ācta, āctum** • Plural: **ācti, āctae, ācta**

vita exculta – civilization – 'improved life'
excultus is a Past Participle of *excolere, excultum* – to cultivate, to improve
aut victor, aut victus – either a winner, or defeated
victus = Past Participle of *vincere, victum* = to conquer, to defeat

elevator << ēlevāre, ēlevātum (to lift)

Alea iacta est. – The die has been cast. Words spoken by Julius Caesar upon crossing the Rubicon in 49 BC, to fight for the leadership of Rome. The phrase *Alea iacta est* came to mean 'the point of no return' – as does the expression 'to cross the Rubicon.'

What is a dictionary?
dictionary << *dictionārius liber* (a saying book) << *dictio* = saying << *dictum*, Past Participle of *dicere, dictum* – to say • In the Middle Ages *dictionārius liber* was a collection of sayings used by university students to study Latin. The first English-Latin dictionary was created by Thomas Elyot in 1538. The first French-Latin dictionary was created by Robert Estienne in 1539.

In English, the same Latin root can form words based on the Present Tense stem or the Past Participle stem. This explains why
B turns into **P** in

describe – description • subscribe – subscription • prescribe – prescription
<< *scrībere, scrīptum*
The Present Tense stem here is *scrib-*, while the Past Participle stem is *script-*.
C turns into **CT** in

produce – production • reduce – reduction • introduce – introduction
<< *dūcere, ductum* = to lead
The Present Tense stem here is *duc-*, while the Past Participle stem is *duct-*.

Here is a list of Latin verbs and their English derivatives formed from both Present Tense and Past Participle stems. These are verbs whose roots are very common in English. Knowing them will help you both to recognize more words and to spell them perfectly.

In the list below I will indicate for each verb
1. the Infinitive form – the form with the ending *-re* in Latin that corresponds to to in English. e.g. *amare* = to love
2. the Past Participle form

Infinitive	Present Participle	Past Participle	
habitāre	*habitāns*	*habitātum*	to live
>> inhabit	>> inhabitant	>> habitation	
fluere	*fluēns*	*flūxum* >> flux	to flow
	>> fluent, fluency, influence, affluence		
	All these words have kept the ē of *fluēns*.		

Infinitive	Present Participle	Past Participle	
mutāre >> mutate, commute, immutable	*mutāns* >> mutant	*mutātum* >> mutation	**to change**
portāre >> deport, import, export	*portāns* >> important	*portātum* >> portative	**to carry**
stāre >> stable	*stāns* >> constant, distant	*statum* >> status	**to stand**
augēre >> augment	*augēns*	*auctum* >> auction	**to increase**
movēre >> move, remove	*movēns*	*motum* >> motion	**to move**
tenēre >> tenacious	*tenēns* >> tenant, content, sustenance	*tentum* >> tentacle, detention	**to hold**
vidēre >> provide	*vidēns*	*visum* >> revise, improvise	**to see**
agēre	*agēns* >> agent	*actum* >> actor	**to do**
capere >> capable	*capiēns*	*captum* >> capture	**to capture**
cēdere >> accede, succeed, proceed, concede, secede	*cēdēns* >> antecedent	*cessum* >> recess, predecessor, process	**to leave**
dūcere >> induce, produce, reduce	*dūcēns*	*ductum* >> deduct, duct, aqueduct, education	**to lead**
iacere	*iaciēns*	*iactum* >> reject, eject, deject, interject, trajectory, subject	**to throw**
legere >> legible	*legēns*	*lectum* >> collect, select	**to read**
pellere >> expel, repel, compel, propel, propeller	*pellēns* >> repellent	*pulsum* >> pulse, pulsate, impulse, compulsion, propulsion, repulsion, expulsion	**to push**
scrībere >> describe, prescribe, proscribe	*scrībēns*	scriptum >> script, scripture, conscription, rescription, description	**to write**
specere >> despicable	*specens*	*spectum* >> respect	**to look at**
solvere >> resolve	*solvēns* >> solvent	*solutum* >> solution, soluble, resolute, resolution, absolute	**to free**

Teneō...

Infinitive	Present Participle	Past Participle	
sedēre >> supersede	*sedēns*	*sessum* >> session	**to sit**
pendēre >> depend	*pendēns* >> pendant	*pēnsum* >> suspense, expense	**to hang**
vertere >> convert, revert	*vertēns*	*versum* >> reverse, converse	**to turn**
pōnere	*pōnēns* >> exponent, exponential	*positum* >> position, pose, composition, composite	**to put**
fīnīre >> finish	*fīniēns*	*fīnītum* >> finite, definite, infinite	**to finish**
sequī	*sequēns* >> sequence, consequence	*sēqūtus* >> consecutive, executive	**to follow**

A Roman legion consisted of soldiers 'collecting' themselves into companies.
legiō, legiōnis, f. (legion)
<< *legere* (to read, to gather)

Veni, vidi, vici. – I came, I saw, I conquered. This is the full text of a message sent by Julius Caesar to the Roman Senate, to describe his battle against King Pharnakles of Pontus near Zela in 47 BC.

convenient
You will always spell this word correctly if you remember that it has *venire* = to come in it. It's the same verb as *veni* in Julius Caesar's *Vēnī, vidi, vici.* – I came, I saw, I conquered.
convenient << *conveniēns* (Present Participle) << *con-* + *venīre* (to come) – 'come together'

MYSTERIES OF MEANING

Noise comes from the Latin... *nausea* = sea sickness!
Did the victims of sea sickness moan and complain so loudly that *nausea* turned into noise? English also kept the original Latin word nausea – sickness >> nauseating, nauseous
Nobody really knows how rosemary came to be called 'rosemary.'
rosmarinus = sea dew >> rosemary • What does it have to do with the sea?
Latin *poena* = punishment arrived in English as pain. Okay, this kinda makes sense.
Poena also exists in English as a law term: subpoena (*sub-* + *poena*) = an order to attend a court

carōta

rosmarinus

allium

Latin High: The *Ex* Files

One day at school Prefix *Ex* was confronted by a bunch of verb bullies. Verb *Rādere Rāsum* (to scrape) said, 'Wanna play with me? Then change your stupid *X* to *R*! I only roll with *R*s!' The bullies knew that many prefixes at Latin High had the habit of changing their last consonant to match the verbs with whom they wanted to be friends. The bullies exploited this weakness to lord it over the prefixes. 'No!' exclaimed *Ex* angrily. 'I don't do your lame consonant gymnastics.' He tried to squeeze past *Rāsum*, but the bully blocked his way. Two more scary-looking verbs approached – *Rumpere Ruptum* (to break) and *Rādīx* (root) nicknamed Radish, known for his radical views. "Show us that *R* or we'll knock your teeth out," growled *Rādīx*. *Rumpere Ruptum* erupted in gleeful laughter. 'Hah-hah,' echoed a voice from behind *Ruptum*'s back. It was Prefix *Con*. Actually, next to *Ruptum* she appeared as *Cor*... as in corrupt.

Ex flashed a scornful smile.
'Leave me alone, you dirty root vegetable,' he told *Rādīx*, getting really annoyed. 'Fix your attitude or we'll erase that smile off your mug real quick.' *Rāsum* pushed *Ex*. At that point *Ex* lost it. He extended his *X* and descended on the bullies with a storm of blows. The bully verbs were on the floor scurrying to haul their vowels when, suddenly, the school principal, Mr. *Lex* popped up out of nowhere, took away *Ex*'s *X* and said angrily, 'Know how to spell expel, Prefix *Ex*?'
'I am sorry, Sir... This will never happen again, Sir... They bullied me...' mumbled *Ex*.

'Mr. *Lex*, he is right! I saw everything!" A hot 9th grader, *Fervere* (to boil), who had a crush on *Ex*, stepped from behind a ficus plant. *Ex* liked her too. There was something effervescent about her. She was effortlessly beautiful.
"*Ex* didn't start the fight, Mr. *Lex*, it's them!" pleaded *Fervere*, pointing at the bullies.
Mr. *Lex* cut her off: 'Being bullied is not an excuse to flatten three Latin verbs. I'll see you tomorrow, Prefix *Ex* – in my office – with your parents!'
Mr. *Lex* whirled around and disappeared taking *Ex*'s *X* with him!

event, eventually << ēvenīre (to happen) << ex (out of) + venīre (to come)

Ex shook his head. His parents were far away somewhere in the steppes of Eurasia working on some 'Proto-Indo-European' language project. Of course, in the end *Ex* got his *X* back, but you still often see him without his *X*. *Ex* appears as *E-* in many English words, but it never participates in 'consonant gymnasics.' That's why we don't have double *RR* in the words formed from the bully verbs erase, erupt, eradicate as well as other words formed with *E-*, such as enormous, elapse, eliminate, elongate, emanate, erode/erosion, and others.

The only time *Ex* ever changes his consonant is when it's followed by *F*. And that's because of his girlfriend, *Ferver*, the Effervescent. effort << *ex- + fortis* (strong)
effect << *ex- + facere* (to do, to make) • efface << *ex- + facies* (face)

More Trouble with Ex-

Prefix *ex-* causes misspells when it is followed by a root starting with *C* – exciting, except, etc. When *C* appears before *E* or *I*, it is pronounced as *S*. As a result, it blends with *ex-* and we can't hear it. Awareness of the Latin origin of words starting with *EXC-* can certainly help with their spelling! Interestingly, the words below arrived in English from Latin with virtually no change in form or meaning.

excite << *excitāre* (to wake up) << *ex-* (out of) + *ciēre* (to set in motion)
exceed, excess << *excēdere, excessum* (to exceed) << *ex- + cēdere, cessum* (to go)
excel << *excellēre* (to excel) << *ex- + cellere* (to move, to rise)
except << *excipere, exceptum* (to take out) << *ex- + capere, captum* (to take, to capture)
excerpt << *excerpere, excerptum* (to select) << *ex- + carpere* (to pluck, to pick)

Latin Word Factories

Some Latin roots produce a lot of words, using prefixes. Clever prefixes attach themselves to whatever stem they can grab – Present Tense or Past Participle.
pōnere = to place, *positum* = placed (Past Participle)
proponent and propose both come from
pōnere = to place –
proponent from the verb's Present Tense stem
propose from its Past Participle stem

Here is a list of the Latin verbs that have contributed the largest number of words in English:

agere, āctum – to do
portāre, portātum – to carry
cēdō, cessum – to go
pōnere, positum – to put, to place
clāmāre, clāmātum – to shout
pressāre, pressātum – to press
currere, cursum – to run
putāre, putātum – to think
dīcere, dictum – to say
regere, rēctum – to rule, to guide
dūcere, ductum – to lead
sistere, statum – to stand
ferre – to bring
spectāre, spectātum – to look
iacere, iactum – to throw
tenēre, tentum – to hold
legere, lēctum – to read
tendere, tentum – to stretch
mittere, missum – to send
vidēre, vīsum – *to see*
pellere, pulsum – to push
vocāre, vocātum – to call
optāre, optātum – to choose
īre, itum – to go

percent
<< per (through)
+ centum (hundred)

Here is a list of prefixes. By the way, most of them also act as prepositions!

a, ab – away from, from
ad – toward, against
ante – before
circum – around
contra – against
con – with
de – not, from
dis – not, against, divide
e, ex – out of, out from
extra – outside
in – in, into, not
inter – between
ob – toward, against
per – through
post – behind, after
pro – for, forward
re – again, against
sub – under, after
super – above
trans – across

example
<< exemplum
<< ex- (from) +
emere (to take, buy)

contagious
<<contāgiō (contact)
<< con- (with) +
tangere (to touch)

And now take a look at these word factories!

pōnere, positum – to put, to place
+ *sub-* >> suppose, + *ob-* >> oppose, + *de-* >> depose, + *ex-* >> expose, + *in-* >> impose

cēdō, cessum – to go
In terms of English spelling, this verb yielded two different models – with *ceed* and with *cede*:
+ *pro-* >> proceed, + *sub* >> succeed, + *ex* >> exceed
+ *re-* >> recede, + *inter-* >> intercede, + *se-* >> secede, + *pre-* >> precede

iacere, iactum – to throw

+ *sub-* >> subject, + *re-* >> reject, + *pro-* >> project, + *ob-* >> object,
+ *de-* >> deject, + *e-* >> eject

ferre – to bring

+ *sub-* >> suffer, + *re-* >> refer, + *de-* >> defer, + *dis-* >> differ, + *ob-* >> offer,
+ *trans-* >> transfer, + *pre-* >> prefer

 vāsum

prevent
<< pre- (before) + venīre (to come)

demonstrate
<< de- (from) + mōnstrāre (to show)

agere, āctum – to do

+ *inter-* >> interact, + *trans-* >> transaction

facere, factum – to do, to make

+ *ad-* >> affect, + *ex-* >> effect, + *per-* >> perfect, + *de-* >> defect, + *in-* >> infect

Please circle the correct spelling:

command / comand   suppresses / supresses
suppervise / supervise   innocent / inocent
occurring / ocurring   addict / adict
propposed / proposed   suggesting / sugesting
deffinition / definition occupation / ocupation
acclaim / aclaim   dissect / disect
ressurrect / resurrect   accommodate / acommodate

connect
<< con- (with) + nectere (to bind)

BIZARRE: PROSE VS VERSE

The abbreviation **VS** stands for the Latin preposition *versus* (against), and is often used when we talk about opposites. • prose *vs* verse = 'prose as opposed to verse'

It is also a legal (law) term used when naming individuals or institutions facing each other in court. **Leo vs Lupus** would refer to a legal battle between a lion and a wolf.

And now let's talk about prose and verse.

Verse is poetry. Not surprisingly, the origin of verse is Latin *versa* – the Past Participle of *vertere* = to turn. A line of poetry doesn't run to the end of the line on the page. It stops and turns to the beginning of the next line! Verse 'turns' to the beginning of the next line.

And now... are you ready for a shocker?

Prose – the opposite of verse – also comes from.... *versus*!

Seriously, at this point, as a Latin teacher, I am rolling my eyes big time.

Why? Well, here we go...prose << *pro-* (forward) + *versa* (turned) = 'turned forward'

The sentences of prose are running forward, toward the end of the line on a page.

They don't turn back toward – to the beginning of – the next line, like verse.

Other English words that have a Latin 'turn' in them include:

adversity, advertise, avert – aversion, divert – diversion, diverse, invert – inversion, controversy, conversation, version, vertical

liber antīquus

ambulance << ambulāre (to walk, move)

By the way, the Roman term for prose was

ōrātiō pedestris = pedestrian speech (as opposed to poetry that has wings to fly!)

LATIN HIGH: DOUBLE CONSONANTS IN PASTS PARTICIPLE STEMS

That morning at Latin High started uneventfully. A bunch of verbs filled the classroom of Mr. *Verbum* (word) who taught Latin Word Studies. Some verbs were yawning. Others were busily digging through their notes.

Salvēte discipulī! (Hello, students!) said Mr. Verbum. *Lūdere Lūsum!*

Lūsum (to play) responded, *Adsum!*

Adsum means 'Present.' It's the 'I' form of the verb *adesse* = to be present << *ad-* + *esse* (to be).

Bene, muttered Mr. Verbum. *Clūdere Clūsum!* (to close)

Adsum!

Cadere Cāsum! (to fall)

Adsum!

gemma

Mr. *Verbum* kept taking attendance, when, suddenly, the Latin High principal, Mr. *Lex* appeared in the doorway, followed by a few kids.

'Mr. *Verbum*, we have some new students joining your class today. Here they are – *Mittere* (to send), *Fatērī* (to admit), and *Quatere* (to shake).'

'Fascinating,' observed Mr. *Verbum*. 'Each has a *T* in the middle of his name!... Okay, may I hear your full names so I can add them to my attendance register...*Mittere*?"

creature << creāre, creātum = "created one"

But just as **Mittere** opened his mouth to say his name, a deep rumble was heard in the distance and the window glass shook.
'Mittttttttt....ttttt.....'
Yes, you guessed it right. By now the classroom, indeed the whole school, was shaking, and the rumble turned into thunder.
What was that? Believe it or not, it was the famous eruption of Mount Vesuvius in AD 79 – the catastrophe that buried the Roman town of Pompeii under ash and debris. Fortunately, Latin High was not located in Pompeii, but the earthquake that accompanied the volcanic eruption rocked the school building like a massive wave would rock a boat.

Mittere kept trying to pronounce his name, but because of all the shaking, his teeth were chattering! 'Mitttttt...ttttere Missssssss.....ssssum.'
'Wow, how many *T*s and *S*s are there in your name?' Mr. **Verbum** was looking at his register. He finally crossed out all the *T*s and *S*s except two *T*s in **Mittere** and 2 *S*s in **Missum**. Other kids also had difficulty saying their names (due to the volcanic eruption). **Fatērī** said his first name just fine, but got stuck on his Past Participle name.
'Fassssssss.....ssssssss.....um.'
The building kept shaking.
'Quatere Quasssssssssssssssssum.'
Mr. **Verbum** crossed out all the *S*s from the kids' last names except two *S* in each name.

culter

Guess what: Ever since the eruption of Vesuvius, Mr. **Verbum** has followed the same rule when spelling kids' names: If your first name has a *T* in the middle, you get **SS** in your participle name! After graduation many of these verbs joined the Roman army, and participated in the Roman conquest of Britain (AD 43-87).
That's why we have those **SS** in many English words.

mittere, missum – to send >> mission, missile, missionary, admit – admission, submit – submission, permit – permission, commit – commission
fatērī, fassum – to admit >> confess, confessor, profess, professor, profession
quatere, quassum – to shake >> discuss, percussion, concussion
sedēre, sessum – to sit >> sedentary, session, possession

mōns ignifer

Interesting, right? And you thought all double consonants in English come from the needy copycat prefixes? No! A lot of them come from the Latin Past Participle stems.

Compare the English words listed on the previous page with those derived from the Latin verbs that have **D** in the Present Tense stem...
vidēre, vīsum – to see << vision, revision
lūdere, lūsum – to play, *collūdere* – to play together << collude, collusion
clūdere, clūsum – to close << conclude, conclusion
fundere, fūsum – to pour, *confunere* – to pour together << confusion, profusion
plaudere, plausum – to clap, applaud << explosion
cadere, cāsum – to fall, *ob-* + *cadere* = *occadere* = to fall together << occasion
See: NO double consonants in the Past Participle stems!

Patience and passion come from the same Latin verb – *patī, passum* = to suffer, but patience is formed from *patī* – the Present Tense stem, while passion is formed from *passum* – the Past Participle.

candēla

cucumīs

PROGRESS AND GOOD GRADES

A real champion of English word creation is the Latin verb *gradī, gressum* – to step, to walk. Both of its stems – the Present Tense *gradī* and the Past Participle *gressum* – have produced piles of English verbs and nouns. Most of them have retained the *grad* and *gress* of the original Latin verb!
gradī >>> grade, degrade, degree, gradation, retrograde, gradient, gradual, graduate, postgraduate
gressum >>> progress, congress, regress, aggression, digress

LAW

Latin *iniūria* (injustice) arrived in English as injury = body damage
Many English words – like injury – come from the Latin *iūs, iūris*, n. = law, right
>> jury, justice, just, jurisdiction, conjure, perjure
Words like conjure, perjure are often misspelled because the *jur* syllable is unstressed.
So remember, there is *iūs, iūris* – the law – in all these English words.

perjure, conjure, adjure << *jūrāre* (to swear) << *jūs, jūris,* n. = law, right
All these words keep the original Latin root *jur*.

iūs, iūris also appears in the Latin legal term
de jūre – by law, how things are supposed to be according to the law
The antonym of this term is
de factō – how things are in actual fact, in real life

idol << *īdōlum* (image, ghost)

Da mihī factum, dabo tibi ius. – Give me the facts, I will give you the law.
(A legal principle of Roman law is that people participating in a lawsuit
should present the facts and the judge will rule on the law that governs them.)
Lex rex. – The law is king. – a principle of government advocating
a rule by law rather than rule by men.

THE BLACK LIST: THE 12 MOST MISSPELLED ENGLISH WORDS OF LATIN ORIGIN

Separate is often misspelled as 'seperate'; definitely is often misspelled as 'definately'....
And now: **The Black List** of scary Latin-origin words that we all have misspelled at some point
in our lives...Today we'll break these word monsters into their Latin components and see if
this helps us to remember their correct spelling once and for all!

radius << *radius* (staff, rod)

1. **Separate**
<< *sēparāre, sēparātum* – to separate << *se-* (self) + *parāre* (prepare)
Separate is built around the stem *para*.
In the adjective separate the stress is on the first syllable. The unstressed vowels in the
pa-ra syllables are not pronounced clearly, causing misspells. But in the verb to separate
and the noun separation you can hear the open-syllable *A* quite clearly. Sometimes, if you
can't figure out the spelling right away, it is helpful to recall other words with the same root.

vōtum sēparātum – an independent ['separate'] vote

2. **Definitely**
<< *de-* (from) + *fīnītus* (final, having an end) • Inside definitely there is *fīnis* = end.

Fīnis corōnat opus. – The end crowns the work.

3. Occurrence
ob- + *currere* (to run) >> *occurrere* >> occur
Occur, concur, recur lose their **RR** in some forms.
There is a special English spelling rule that helps us remember when this happens.

> No 'dino' in denominator!
> denominator << *de* (from, down)
> + *nōminātum* (named)

The double consonant rule for the last consonant of the root:
If the root syllable is stressed, and there is an ending following it, we get double consonants.
Our root is *cur*, and whenever it is followed by *-ed, -ing, -ence*, the **R** doubles:
occurred, occurring, occurrence • recurred, recurring, recurrence
concurred, concurring, concurrence
If the syllable is unstressed, or if there is no ending after the root, there is no consonant doubling.
The root *cur* is stressed, but there is no ending following it – no **RR**: occur, recur, concur
Root *fer* is unstressed – no **RR**: reference, preference, conference, offered, offering

4. Consensus
con- (together) + *sēnsus* (agreement) << *sentīre, sēnsum* – to feel
sēnsus is a masculine Latin noun with the standard masculine ending *-us.*
It is derived from *sēnsum* – the Past Participle of the verb *sentīre*. It's about the 'feeling' of being in agreement, and it is related to other English words that came from the Latin
sentīre >> sense, sensible, sensation, sensor
Consensus has nothing to do with census (counting and listing the inhabitants of a country).
Roman *cēnsus* (listing the names and property assessments of all Roman citizens) comes from the verb *cēnsēre, cēnsum* – to count, to assess.

Qui tacet cōnsentīre vidētur. – He who is silent appears to consent. – 'Silence gives consent.'
tacēre, tacitum – to be silent • *vidētur* = is seen (a Passive Voice form of *vidēre, vīsum* = to see)

5. Necessary
<< *necessārius* (necessary) << *ne* (not) + *cēdere, cessum* – to go, to leave
A necessary thing is something that we don't want to go away.
No **CC** in necessary! That's because the prefix *ne-* ends in a vowel,
and doesn't participate in consonant gymnastics.

The **SS** in *cess* comes from the Past Participle *cessum*.
If you add *pro-* (forward) to *cess*, you get process!
If you add *re-* (back) to *cess*, you get recess!
If you add *in-* (not) to *cess*, you get incessant!
If you add *sub-* (under, after) to *cess*, you get success!
That's right, success is what comes after you leave
on a mission – it's the result of an action.

Necesse est = is necessary
Currere necesse est. – It is necessary to run.
Labōrāre necesse est. – It is necessary to work.

Avēs volant.

cancellation
<< *cancellāre* (to cross out)
<< *carcer* (prison, crossed bars)

6. Acceptable
No **X** in acceptable!
ad- (toward) + *capere* (to take) >> *acceptāre* = to receive
The moment you see *ac-* watch out for double **CC**!!!!
It's that silly prefix *ad-* doing its favorite sport – the 'consonant gymnastics'!

ferre

7. Referred
There is no **FF** in referred/preferred because prefixes *re-* and *pre-*
end in a vowel so they don't do 'consonant gymnastics.'
referred << *re-* + *ferre* (to bring, to carry) = *referre* – to bring back

referre

refer, prefer, and confer lose **RR** in some forms. Apply **'The double consonant
rule for the last consonant of the root'** (from the previous page):
If the root *fer* is stressed, and there is an ending following it, we have double consonants:
referring, referred • preferring, preferred • conferring, conferred
If the *fer* root is unstressed, or if there is no ending after the root, no doubling:
refer, prefer, confer • reference, preference, conference

praeferre

8. Particularly
<< *particularis* – having to do with a small part
<< *particula* – particle, small part

Latin suffix **-cula** is a diminutive suffix. Diminutive suffixes carry the meaning of something small or cute. In English we use **-ie** or **-y** to make a noun sound smaller: kitty, doggy, meanie

Some English words have kept their Latin suffix **-cul/-cula**
molecule << **mōles** (weight) + **-cula** = of little weight
minuscule << **minusculus** << **minus** (smaller) + **cul** = extremely small
ridicule << **ridiculus** << **rīdēre** (to laugh) + **-cul** = laughable, very funny
particle << **pars** (part) + **-cul** = tiny piece
muscle << **mūs** (mouse) + **-cul** = a little mouse (when you flex a muscle it looks like 'a mouse' moving under your skin)
formula << **fōrma** (form) + **-ula** = little form

motor << movēre, mōtum (to move)

9. Conscience

<< **con-** (together) + **scīre** (to know)
Have you noticed that there is science in conscience?
That's because both these words come from the Latin **scīre** = to know.
Scīre is a wonderful verb to know, because it appears in quite a few English words, causing them to display the **SC** spelling:
science, conscience, conscious, omniscience (**omni** = all), conscientious
To remember the spelling of conscience, think of the Latin word **scientia** = knowledge.

Scientia potestās est. – Knowledge is power.
Sine scientia ars nihil est. – Without knowledge, skill (*ars*) is nothing.

The antonym of *scīre* is *nescīre* = to not know • *Sciō!* – I know! • *Nesciō!* – I don't know!

10. Accommodate

Here we have two champions of the Latin Consonant Gymnastics Junior League – prefixes **ad-** and **con-**. **Ad-** before **C** turns into **acc-**. **Con-** before **M** turns into **com-** and we end up with two consonant doubles!!!
Compare accommodate with recommend: **re-** ends in a vowel, so it doesn't participate in 'consonant gymnastics.' That's why there is no **CC** in recommend or reconnect.

11. Experience
<< *ex-* (out of) + *perīrī, pertum* (to try)
>> experience, expert, expertise, experiment all share the *peri/pert* root.
Latin *experientia* means 'experience' or 'experiment.'
Experientia docet. – Experience teaches.

pollution << polluere (to make dirty)
<< por-/pol (for) + luere (to smear)

12. Millennium
<< *mīlle* (thousand) + *annus* (year)
Both doubled consonants in millennium come from the word roots.
In English we find *mille* in measure terms:
millimeter (1000 in a meter), milliliter (1000 in a liter), milligram (1000 in a kilogram)
Also: millipede (1000 feet) and million.
Million appeared only in 13th and 14th century Italy.
The ancient Greeks had no name for numbers greater than ten thousand.
The Romans had no name for numbers higher than a hundred thousand.
Annus – year appears in annual, biannual, biennial, perennial.

LATIN CARDINAL NUMERALS

Here are some Latin cardinal numerals and number prefixes that often appear in English. (I am keeping my fingers crossed that you remember the difference between cardinal and ordinal numerals!)

No get in negative!
negative
<< negāre, negātum (to deny)

1. *ūnus / uni-*
>> unite • universe (<< *vertere, versum* = to turn)
>> uniform (<< *fōrma* = shape) • unilateral (<< *latus* = side)
Unus vir, nūllus vir. – One man is no man (strength is in numbers).
vir, virī, m. – man • *nūllus* = none >> null, annul, annulment

NULL & VOID

2. *duo / bi-*
>> binoculars (<< *oculus* = eye) • bipartisan (<< *partīre* = to divide)
>> bicameral (<< *camera* = room) • bilingual (<< *lingua* = language)
>> biceps (<< *-ceps,* form of *caput* = head; biceps = a 'two-headed' muscle that has 2 points of attachment)

Bis dat qui cito dat. – He gives twice who gives quickly.

bis = twice • *dat* << he/she/it gives << *dare, datum* – to give • *qui* = who

1,000,000,000,000 = one million million

3. *trēs / tri-*
>> triangle, triceps, trillion, triple, triplet, trident (*tri-* + *dēns, dentis*, m.– tooth)

4. *quattuor / quadri-*
>> quadrilateral (<< *latus* = side), quadrant, quadruplets

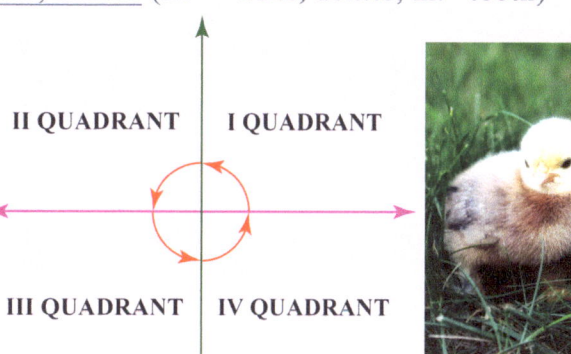

5. *quīnque / quint-*
>> quintessential, quintet

WHAT DO ONION AND UNION HAVE IN COMMON?

They both come from the Latin *ūnus* – one! One of the words derived from *ūnus* is *ūniō* = an onion. A garlic can be separated into cloves, but an onion can not – it's ONE! Somehow, through the centuries, union came to mean unity, while onion – became a vegetable. It could have been the other way around.

Imagine,

instead of the **Union Jack** (the British flag) we could have had the **Onion Jack**!
(or, even better, the **Garlic Jack** – since the United Kingdom consists of a few 'cloves' – England, Scotland, etc.)

instead of the **European Union** – we would have had a tasty **European Onion**!
(It's not for no reason that the iconic soup of France is an onion soup!)

instead of the **United States of America** – the **Garlic States of America** (50 cloves!)

By the way, onions originated in Egypt where they were treated with reverence, as the symbol of the many-layered universe. Egyptians even swore oaths on onions.

The Difference between Biannual and Biennial

biannual = occurring twice a year << *bi-* (two) + *annus* (year)
biennial = occurring once in 2 years << *biennium* (a 2-year period) << *bi-* (two) + *annus* (year)
So in botany,
an annual plant grows from a seed and dies within one year;
a perennial plant grows from a seed and lives for many years;
a biennial plant has a life cycle of 2 years.
perennial << *perennis* (durable, lasting for years) << *per-* (through) + *annī* (plural of *annus*)

A Man of Three Letters

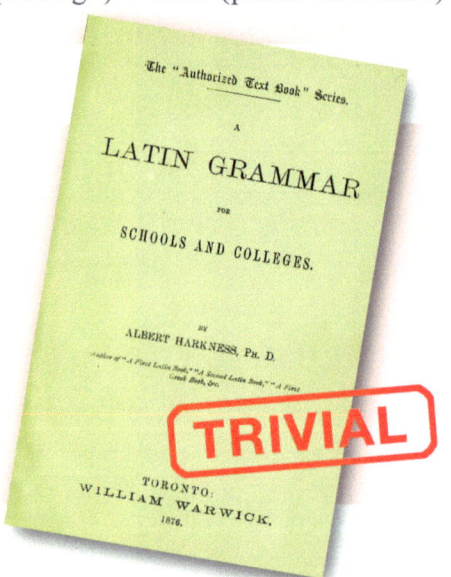

You know what a **euphemism** is? It's an indirect way of stating a truth that may otherwise upset someone.
Instead of fat you may refer to a person as full-bodied.
Instead of He died you may want to say He passed on.
So, the Roman euphemism for thief was
homo trium literarum = 'a man of three letters,' because thief in Latin is *fūr*.

Why is Trivial - 'Boring'?

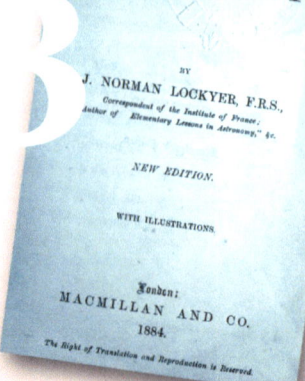

Trivial means 'banal, uninteresting, common, boring." This word comes from the Latin
trivium – 'a place where three roads meet.' The Romans worshiped the goddess of crossroads –
trivius dea – the 'goddess of three ways.'
In the Middle Ages university students chose between
two courses of study – *trivium* and *quadrivium*.
Trivium included 3 subjects – grammar, logic, and rhetoric.
Quadrivium included 4 subjects – music, arithmetic, geometry, and astronomy.
Quadrivium was a more prestigious course than *trivium*.
That's why trivial means 'uninteresting, boring.'
Trivia is the plural of *trivium*. Around 1965 Trivia emerged
as the name of a game popular in colleges –
a contest where participants answer questions about popular culture.

What are the Essences in Quintessential?

quintessential << *quint essentia* = the fifth essence

Ancient Greeks believed that the world was made of four elements – earth, water, fire, and air. Aristotle added a fifth element, or 'essence,' to this list – ether, that was said to be the purest element. It was believed to be bright, indestructible, and capable of circular motion.

Extracting ether was one of the main goals of medieval alchemy.

This is how the 'fifth essence' came to mean 'the purest substance,' or 'the most essential part.'

Latin Ordinal Numerals

1. *prīmus* – first
>> primal, prima, primacy, primary, prime minister, primitive, primate, primordial, subprime
2. *secundus* – second >> second, secondary
3. *tertius* – third >> tertiary
4. *quārtus* – fourth >> quart, quarter, quartet

hour << **hōra** (hour, time)
minute << **minūtus** (small)
second << **secundus** (next)
<< **secunda pars minūta**
(the next small part)

Moving on to even bigger numbers! Cardinal – ordinal:

10. *decem – decimus* >> dean, December
100. *centum – centesimus* >> cent, century, centurion, centennial
1000. *mīlle – mīllesimus* >> million, mile, millipede, millennial

There Will Be Consequences!

The Latin verb *sequī, sēcūtum* (to follow) gave us a load of English words. Some are tricky to spell, but they become easy if you remember that all of them have the *seq / sec* root. Some English words were formed from the Present Tense stem *sequī*:

sequence, consequence, subsequent, sequel

Another bunch of words was derived from the Past Participle stem *sēcūtum*:

persecute, execute, prosecute

Guess what else came from *sēcūtum*... second! Because second follows the first!

So just remember that all these words, from sequence to prosecute have a second in them – and you'll never misspell them again!

It's So Complicated, I am Perplexed and Frustrated!

Have you noticed the suspicious *pl / bl* in such words as
simple, double, triple, quadruple, multiple
What's with that *pl*?
Even more mysterious:
You find the same *pl* in complex and complicated...
Now, please, don't tell me that simple and complex come from the same word!
Uh-oh... They do!
The key to the mystery is the word pliable – a quality of being easy to fold or modify.
All these *pl* words come from
plicāre, plicātum (to fold) • *plectere, plexum* (to fold, to weave, to tangle).

> frustrated
> << *frūstrāre, frūstrātum*
>   (to deceive, to disappoint)
> << *frūstrā* (adverb) = in vain,
>   with no result

simple = folded once (root *sem* = one / as one, together with); double = folded twice;
triple = folded thrice; quadruple = folded 4x; multiple = folded many times!
complex << *con-* + *plectere, plexum* (to fold, to weave, to tangle)
complicated << *con-* + *plicāre, plicātum* (to fold)

When you comply with rules, you fold yourself in this or that way to accommodate the rules!
A display is something unfolded and presented to your eyes.
implicit = folded in • explicit = folded out
imply = to express and idea in a veiled, 'folded-in' way
perplexed = puzzled to the degree of being all tangled up!

Latin Adjectives: Comparative Degrees

To compare the qualities of objects, we use the **Comparative** and **Superlative degrees of adjectives**. For example:

Adjective: high – *altus*
Comparative degree: higher – *altior* (masculine, feminine), *altius* (neuter)
Superlative degree: the highest – *altissimus* m., *altissima* f., *altissimum* n.

ferre, lātum = to carry

superlative << *super* (over, beyond) + *lātum* (carried)

To form Comparative degrees, use suffixes
-ior for masculine and feminine forms of adjectives • *-ius* for neuter forms of adjectives

Omnia dicta fortiora si dicta Latina. – Everything said [is] stronger if said in Latin.
omnia – plural neuter form of *omnis* = all
dictum – 'said' is a past participle of *dīcere*, *dictum* – to say; plural neuter – *dicta*
fortiora – plural neuter form of *fortior* – comparative degree of *fortis* = strong

To form Superlative degrees, use suffixes *-issimus, -issima, -issimum*

clarus – bright, *clarior* – brighter, *clarissimus* – the brightest
brevis – short, *brevior* – shorter, *brevissimus* – the shortest

optimus

bonus

melior

Some adjectives don't follow these rules and form irregular comparative and superlative degrees. These are the most frequently used adjectives, and it's not surprising that it's these irregular forms that we use almost every day in English. Take a look at this list!

good – ***bonus, bona, bonum***
better – ***melior*** (m.f.), ***melius*** (n.) • the best – ***optimus, optima, optimum***
>>> English: bonus, optimum, optimal (the best), ameliorate (to improve something)
Optima medicīna temperantia est. – Self-control is the best medicine.
Usus est optimus magister. – Experience is the best teacher.
ūsus, ūsūs, m. = use, experience, habit

fungus maior et fungus minor

big – ***magnus, magna, magnum*** • bigger – ***maior*** (m.,f.), ***maius*** (n.)
the biggest – ***maximus, maxima, maximum***
>>> English: major, maximum, maxim (a wise saying), maxi- (prefix)
Hodiē nūllus, crās maximus. – Today nobody, tomorrow the greatest.
hodiē = today (adverb) • *crās* = tomorrow (adverb)

little – ***parvus***
less – ***minor*** (m.,f.), ***minus*** (n.) • the least – ***minimus, minima, minimum***
>>> English: minor, minus, minimum, minimal, minimalist, mini- (prefix)

Qui invidet, minor est. – He who envies, is smaller (betrays his inferiority).
invidēre, invīsum = to envy, to be jealous

bad – *malus, mala, malum*
worse – *peior* (m., f.), *peius* (n.) • the worst – *pessimus, pessima, pessimum*
>>> English: pejorative (negative), pessimistic (hopeless), pessimism (hopelessness)

much, many – *multus, multa, multum*
more – *plus* (m., f., n.) • most – *plurimus, plurima, plurimum*
>>> English: plus, plural, plurality

pessimist

Plus vident oculī quam oculus. – [Two] eyes see more than one eye
(about people helping each other). • *quam* = than • *oculus, oculī,* m. = an eye

above, on top – *superus, supera, superum*
higher – *superior* (m.,f.), *superius* (n.)

optimist

the highest – *suprēmus / summus, suprēma / summa, suprēmum / summum*
>>> English: superior, superb, supreme, sum, summit

the last, the most extreme – *ulter – ulterior – ultimus*
>>> English: ultimatum, ultra- (prefix)

multiplication << multi + plicāre, plicātum (to fold up)

old – *senex* (m., f., n.)
older – *senior* (m., f.), *senius* (n.) • the oldest – *senissimus, senissima, senissimum*
>> English: senior, seniority, senile (forgetful because of old age), senility

located outside – *exterus, extera, exterum*
even further outside – *exterior* (m., f.), *exterius* (n.)
outermost, last – *extremus, extrema, extremum*
>>> English: exterior, extreme, extremist, extremal

**irresistible
<< irresistibilis
<< in- (not) + re- (against) +
sistere (take a stand)**

low – *īnferus, īnfera, īnferum*
lower – *īnferior, īnferius* • the lowest – *īnfimus*
>>> English: inferior, inferiority

iocus (a joke) >> ioculus (a small joke) >> jocular

next – *posterus*
later – *posterior* (m., f.), *posterius* (n.) • last – *postumus*
>>> English: posterior (located behind; noun – a person's butt!) posthumous (after death)
Posthumous really does come from the Latin *postumus* "last," but at some point
an *H* was inserted into this word, because people started associating it with
humus = earth and the Latin verb *humare* = to bury.

located above – *superus, supera, superum*
even higher – *superior* (m., f.), *superius* (n.) • the highest, at the top – *supremus/summus*
>>> English: superior, superiority, supreme, sum, summary

first – *primus*
earlier, before – *prior* (m., f.), *prius* (n.)   angulus (corner, angle) >> angular
>> English: priority, prior
a priori – a conclusion made based on theoretical knowledge, not on experience

Using the adjectives above and the forms of the verb *esse* (to be), please translate
the following sentences. Remember that Latin adjectives (including their comparative and
superlative degrees) echo the gender and number of the nouns they describe.

Mount Olympus (*Mōns Olympus* m.) is high, Mount Vesuvius (*Mōns Vesuvius* m.) is lower.
The last (the farthest out) island (*īnsula* f.) is the smallest.
A star (*stella* f.) is bright, but (*sed*) the Moon (*Luna* f.) is brighter.
A river (*flumen* n.) is good, but the sea (*mare* n.) is the best.
The magician (*magus* m.) is evil, but the witch (*malefica* f.) is the worst.
Many temples (*templum* n.) are ancient/old (*antiquus*).   circulus
Jupiter is the top/highest god (*deus* m.)   >> circular
The grandmother (*ava* f.) is old, but the grandfather (*avus* m.) is older.

polus (axis, sky) >> polar

lūna >> lunar

stella >> stellar

līnea (a string) >> linear

A Pie in the Sky

Do you like pies? How about a pecan pie, an apple pie, a key lime pie?
If you do, don't be shocked at the strange origin of pie! Here we go:
The word pie comes from the Latin name of a bird – *pīca* = a magpie.
Magpies are birds that have a terrible reputation for stealing and collecting in their nests all sorts of shiny objects. They – allegedly! – steal spoons and forks, jewelry, coins, nails, and whatnot! At some point the word *pīca* acquired the meaning of 'a collection of odd random objects.' From here it was just a step to a pastry that contains all sorts of ingredients (apples, nuts, berries, etc.)
So 'pie in the sky' is real, after all!

Pīca syrēnem imitāns! – A magpie imitating a siren! (a Roman saying about a person who can't sing but insists on singing – a reference to the enchanting songs of sirens, magical creatures of the ancient Greek mythology) • *imitārī, imitātum* = to imitate

Latin Adverbs

Latin adverbs come with a variety of endings, but the most common is *-e.*
bonus – good; *bene* – well
If, in class, you give me the correct answer, I'd say *Bene!* – 'Good!'
malus – bad, evil; *male* – poorly, badly
bene and *male* appear as prefixes in many English words.
If you remember the *E* in *bene*, you won't misspell benediction, benefactor, benefit, beneficial.
bene- + *dicere* (say) >> benediction (blessing)
bene- + *facere* (do) >> benefactor

spectrum malīgnum

benevolent = *bene-* + *volo* (I want) = 'of good will'
male- + *facere* (do) >> maleficent (evil-doer)
male- + *facere* (do) via French *faisant* (doing) >> malfeasance (wrongdoing)
male- + *gen* (give birth) >> *malignus* >> malignant
also malice, malware, malfunction, maladjusted, malaria, malformed, and more...

Poenitentia sēra rārē vēra. – Late repentance is rarely sincere.
sērus = late • *rārē* = rarely – an adverb • *vērus* = true

Let's use these Latin adverbs!
"How are you?" in Latin is
Quid agis? = 'What do you do?'
Agis = you do << ***agere*** – to do
Response:
Bene – Well, doing well, or ***Male*** – Not good
Quid agis?

Even though ***nihil*** is 'nothing' it managed to squeeze itself into some English words:
annihilation (complete destruction)
<< ***ad-*** (toward) + ***nihil*** (nothing)
nihilism (the rejection of all religious and moral principles)

refrigerator << re- (again) + **frīgerāre, frīgerātum (to make cold)**

'Thank you', in Latin, is: ***Gratias***.
The response to 'thank you' can be ***Libenter*** (adverb) – Gladly, ***Certe*** (adverb) – Certainly or, if they thank you for a favor, you can say, ***Nihil est*** – It's nothing.

Some Latin adverbs came into English unchanged
grātīs – for free • ***interim*** – meanwhile • ***quondam*** – formerly, in the past
tandem – in Latin: at last, so much; in English – one after another, side-by-side
verbatim – word for word << ***verbum*** – word
Some Latin adverbs turned into nouns in English:
aliās – another time >> English: alias – a different name
alibi – somewhere else >> English: alibi – evidence that
a person was not at the scene of the crime when the crime was committed

Frīgidum est!

CANDID, CANDIDATE, CANDLE, AND CANDY

A candidate was candid about eating some candy by the light of a candle....
Candid and candidate come from Latin ***candidus*** = bleached, shiny, white
Men running for government elections in Ancient Rome wore bleached super-white togas to indicate the purity of their character and intentions. Such a toga was called ***toga candida***.
A man who wore ***toga candida*** was called ***candidātus*** = a candidate.
The adjective ***candidus*** comes from ***candēre*** = to shine
The root ***cand*** is found in candle, candelabra, incandescent, incense, etc.
So, yes, candidate and candle have something in common – they shine!
As for candy, it comes from the ancient Persian root ***quand*** = sugar, shiny crystal.
We find a similar root in Sanskrit, the language of ancient India – ***khanda*** = sugar.

Etymologists normally don't associate *cand* = shiny with *khand* = sugar, but don't you think these words could come from the same, even more ancient, source – the Proto-Indo-European language that gave birth to the family of Indo European languages to which Latin, Persian, and Sanskrit all belong?

LATIN LANDSCAPE

Take a look at this beautiful landscape! I indicate the plural for the nouns that use the plural *-es* ending. All other nouns have the regular plural endings *-i, -ae, -a.*

āēr, āeris, m – air >> aerial, aerate, aerodynamics • *caelum, caelī,* n. – sky >> celestial, ceiling
nūbēs, nūbis, f. – cloud; plural: *nūbēs* >> nebular, nebula • *sōl, sōlis,* m. – sun >> solar, solarium

lūna, lūnae, f. – moon >> lunar, lunatic
campus, campī, m. – field >> camp, campus, campaign
silva, silvae, f. – forest >> Pennsylvania, Sylvia
herba, herbae, f. – grass >> herbal, herbivore, herbaceous
arbor, arbōris, f. – tree; plural: *arbōrēs* >> arboreal, arboretum
flōs, flōris, m. – flower; plural: *flōrēs* >> flower, floral, florid, florist
flūmen, flūminis, n. – river • *rīvus, rīvī,* m. – small stream, brook << river, riviera
mōns, montis, m.– mountain, hill; plural: *montēs* << mountain, Montana

pixel – not from Latin!
pictures >> pics >> pix
+ el (first 2 letters of element)
>> pixel

Use the following adjectives and the verb *esse* (to be) to make sentences.
Example: A brook/river is cold. – ***Rīvus frīgidus est.***
Remember, Latin adjectives copycat
the gender and the number of nouns.
albus – white >> album
viridis – green
clarus – bright >> Clara, declare, clarify, eclair
ruber – red >> rubric, ruby
magnus – big >> magnitude, magnanimous
parvus – small
frīgidus – cold >> frigid, refrigerator
altus – high >> altitude

Clouds are white.
The Sun is bright.
The Moon is white.
The grass is green.
Flowers are red.
The forest is large.
The trees are small.
The air is cold.
The mountain is high.
Rivers are large.

No ant in apparently!!!
<< appārēns (appearing)

GENETIVE CASE

The English language uses prepositions to connect nouns to other words. For example, in 'a friend of a friend', the preposition of shows the connection between the two friends. In Latin, instead of a preposition, we convey the same idea with an ending attached to a noun:
amīcus amīcī = friend of a friend

amīcus is the main form of a noun called the Nominative Case.
amīcī = 'of a friend' is a form called the Genitive Case.
Genitive case typically carries the idea of belonging. English phrases like 'a friend of the king,' 'leg of a chair,' 'day of my birth' (birthday) are translated into Latin by using the Genitive case of the noun coming after of.

RUBRIC (a heading on a document) << ruber (red)

GEN. US, R, UM → ī   A → AE

Masculine nouns ending in *-us* or *-r* and neuter nouns ending in *-um* change their endings to *-ī* in Genitive Case. Feminine nouns ending in *-a* change their endings to *-ae.*

liber discipulī = a book of a student (or 'student's book')
discipulus – Nominative Case, *discipulī* – Genitive Case
cauda cattī – the tail of a cat
cattus – Nominative Case, *cattī* – Genitive Case
terrae mōtus = earthquake ('movement of the earth')
terrae is the Genitive case of *terra* = earth
impetus animī = enthusiasm ('movement of the soul')
animī is the Genitive case of *animus* = mind, soul
nihilī homo = a worthless person ('man of nothing')
nihilī is the Genitive case of *nihil* n. = nothing
Sic trānsit glōria mundī. – So ends the earthly glory.
trānsīre, trānsitum – to go over, to cross >> transit, transition, transient, transitory
glōria = glory >> glory, glorious, glorify
mundī – the Genitive case of *mundus, mundī,* m. = world >> mundane
Dīves aut inīquus, aut inīquī haeres. – A rich man is either a wrongdoer, or an heir of a wrongdoer (Roman proverb).
dīves = rich • *inīquī* = the Genitive case of *inīquus* = unjust >> iniquity (injustice)
haeres, haeredis, f.,m. – heir / heiress >> heir, heiress, hereditary, heredity

crocodīlus

Cauda crocodīlī longa est.
Cauda pavī māgnifica est.

pavus

ACCUSATIVE CASE

Videō folium.
Folium viridis est.

The Accusative case is associated with what is called the **direct object**, that is, when the action of a verb directly involves a noun: I see him... I accuse her... In English only pronouns have Accusative Case forms. For example, we say 'He plays' but 'I see him.' 'He' is a **subject** pronoun, and 'him' is an **object** pronoun. Subject – Object: She – her, we – us, they – them.

In Latin every noun has an 'object' form – the Accusative Case form. Masculine nouns ending in *-us* and *-r*, change their ending to *-um* in the Accusative case. Feminine nouns ending in *-a* change their endings to *-am.* Neuter nouns ending in *-um* don't change in the Accusative case.

Videō cattum. – I see a cat. • *Videō amīcum.* – I see a friend.
Nominative case: *cattus, amīcus* • Accusative Case: *cattum, amīcum*

Videō cattum.
Oculī cattī viridēs sunt.

ACC. US, R → UM   A → AM
UM → UM

Arēnam metiris! – You count the sand! (Roman saying about a useless activity)

arēnam is Accusative Case of *arēna, arēnae,* f. = sand • *mētīrī, mēnsum* = to measure

Ars amat fortūnam et fortūna artem. – Art loves fortune, and fortune loves art.

artem = Accusative case of *ars, artis,* f. = art

fortūnam = Accusative case of *fortūna, fortūnae,* f. = fortune, luck, wealth

Manus manum lavat. – One hand washes the other (about people exchanging favors).

manum = Accusative case of *manus, manūs,* f. = hand

lavāre, lavātum = to wash >> lavatory, laundry

Qui male agit, odit lucem. – He who does evil hates the light (criminals prefer secrecy).

agere, āctum = to act • *ōdisse, ōsum* = to hate • *lūcem* – Acc. case of *lūx, lūcis,* f. = light

Si vīs pācem, parā bellum. – If you want peace, prepare [for] war.

(Being strong prevents an attack.) • *pācem* – Accusative case of *pāx, pācis,* f. = peace

bellum – Accusative case of *bellum, bellī,* n.= war >> belligerent

velle = to want • parāre, parātum = prepare

Necessitās nōn habet lēgem. – Need has no law (poverty can drive people to unlawful actions).

lēgem – Accusative case of *lēx, lēgis,* f. = law • *habēre, habitum* = to have

Qui pingit florem, non pingit floris odorem. –

He who paints a flower can't paint the scent/smell of the flower.

pingere, pictum = to paint • *odōrem* – Accusative case of *odor, odōris,* m. = smell

flōrem – Accusative case, *flōris* – the Genitive case of *flōs, flōris,* m. = flower

Qui tōtum vult, totum perdit. – He who wants it all, loses it all.

('Grasp no more than your hand will hold.') • *velle* – to want, wish

tōtum – Accusative case of *tōtum* n. = the whole • *perdere, perditum* = to lose

Cōgnātiō movet invidiam. – Acquaintance (knowing someone personally) produces envy.

invidiam = Accusative case of *invidia, invidiae,* f. = envy

movēre, mōtum = to move, to agitate

Cōnscientia crimen prōdit. – Conscience betrays guilt. ('Conscience issues its verdict'.)

crīmen, crīminis, n. = judgment, verdict • *prōdere, prōditum* – to produce, to betray

Lepōris vītam vivit. – He lives the life of a rabbit (about a person who lives in fear).

lepōris = Genitive case of *lepor, lepōris,* m. = rabbit, hare

vītam = Accusative case of *vīta, vītae,* f. = life >> vital, vitality • *vīvere, vīctum* = to live

Lingua lāpsa vērum dicit. – A slipping tongue tells the truth (unguarded speech reveals the truth).

lingua, linguae, f. – tongue, language • *lāpsus* – slipping, uncontrolled

vērum – Accusative case of *vērum* n. – true, truth

umbram suam metuēns – afraid of one's own shadow (about fearful people)
umbram – Accusative case of *umbra, umbrae*, f. = shadow
suam – Accusative case, f. of the pronoun *suus* = his/her own
metuēns – Present Participle of *metuere, metūtum* = to fear

Habeō cāseum!

Two Ways to Say 'I Have'

The Latin verb *habēre, habitum* = to have is similar to the English 'have.'
A direct object following this verb is always an Accusative case form of a noun or adjective.
Habeō equum. – I have a horse. << *equus, equī*, m. = horse

↳ Acc.case

So now you know two ways to say 'I have / you have / etc.' in Latin:
1. *Est mihī stylus.* – 'Is to me a pen.'
2. *Habeō stylum.* – I have a pen.

Est mihi cāseus!

Dative Case

Dative case often describes direction: 'to a friend' will be translated into Latin as *amīcō*, with the Dative case ending *-ō*. The word 'Dative' comes from the Latin verb *dare, datum* = to give • *Dō amīcō...* – I give to a friend... • *Dīcō amīcō...* – I say to a friend... Maculine nouns ending in *-us, -r* and neuter nouns engins in *-um* change their ending to *-o* in the Dative case. Feminine nouns ending in *-a* change their ending to *-ae.*

cāseus

Deō gratias – thank God • *Deō* – Dative case of *deus, deī*, m. – god
Verbum sapientī sat. – A word is sufficient to a wise [person].('A word to the wise is sufficient.')
verbum, verbī, n. = word • *sapientī* – Dative case of *sapiēns* = wise
Dā dextram miserō. – Give/offer a hand to a man in trouble.
dare, datum = to give • *miserō* = Dative case of *miserus* = miserable, poor
dextram = Accusative case of *dextra, dextrae*, f. = right hand >> dexterity, ambidextrous
Expertō crēde! – Believe/trust an expert! • *expertō* is Dative case of *expertus* = expert
Flamma fūmō est proxima. – Fire is next to smoke. ('Where there's smoke, there's fire.')
flamma, flammae, f. = flame • *fūmō* = Dative case of *fūmus, fūmī*, m. = smoke >> to fume, fumes
Homō hominī aut deus, aut lupus. – Man is to man either a god or a wolf (people either admire or hate one another). • *hominī* = Dative Case of *homō, hominis*, m. = man, human

DAT.   US, R, UM → O   A → AE

Ignem īgnī ne addas! – Don't add fire to fire! (don't cause trouble)

īgnem = Accusative case, and *īgnī* = Dative case of *īgnis, īgnis,* m.= fire

addere, additum = to add << *ad-* (to, toward) + *dare* (to give) >> add, addition

marī aquam addere – to add water to the sea • *marī* – Dative case of *mare, maris,* n. = sea

aquam – Accusative case of *aqua, aquae,* f. = water

ABLATIVE CASE

ABL. US, R, UM → ō   A → Ā

The Latin Ablative case can be translated into English using the prepositions <u>with</u>, <u>by</u>, and <u>in</u>.

I write with a pen. – *Scrībō stylō.*

a book written by a friend... *liber scrīptus amīcō.*

Masculine nouns ending in *-us* or *-r* and neuter nouns ending in *-um* change their endings to *-ō* in the Ablative case. Feminine nouns ending in *-a* keep their ending (except *-a* becomes long: *-ā).*

annō Dominī – in the year of [Our] Lord

The abbreviation <u>A.D.</u> is used to indicate dates in relation to the date of Jesus Christ's birth.

annō – Ablative case of *annus, annī,* m. = year

Dominī – Genitive case of *dominus, dominī,* m. – lord

bonā fidē – in good faith • *bonā fidē* – Ablative case of *bona fidēs* = good faith << <u>fidelity</u>

malum malō medicāre – to cure evil by evil • *malum* = Accusative case of *malum* = n. evil

malō = Ablative case – 'with/by evil' • *medicāre, medicātum* = to heal

FIVE LATIN CASES

And now take a look all the case endings together for masculine nouns ending in *-us, -r,* feminine nouns ending in *-a* and neuter nouns ending in *-um*:

			masculine	feminine	neuter
Nominative	a friend, a temple		*amīcus*	*amīca*	*templum*
Genitive	of a friend, of a temple		*amīcī*	*amīcae*	*templī*
Dative	to a friend, to a temple		*amīcō*	*amīcae*	*templō*
Accusative	[I see] a friend / temple	[*videō*]	*amīcum*	*amīcam*	*templum*
Ablative	by a friend, by a temple		*amīcō*	*amīcā*	*templō*

> ***Dum spīrō spērō.*** –
> While I breathe, I hope.

Dō dōnum amīcae. – I give a gift to a (girl) friend.
dōnum is the Accusative case of ***dōnum*** • ***amīcae*** is the Dative case of ***amīca***
Neuter nouns have the same forms in the Nominative and Accusative cases.
Videō caudam cattī. – I see the tail of a cat.
caudam is the Accusative case of ***cauda*** • ***cattī*** is the Genitive case of ***cattus***
Scrībō plumbō. – I write with a pencil. • ***plumbō*** is the Ablative case of ***plumbum*** = pencil

In the following sentences please indicate the case of each noun.
Audit fābulam vītae meae. – He hears the story of my life.
fābula f. – story • ***vīta mea*** f. – my life
Dā librum discipulō. – Give the book to the student.
liber m. – book • ***discipulus*** m. – student
Orātiō ōrātōre scripta est. – The speech is written by the speaker.
ōrātiō f. – speech • ***ōrātor*** m. – orator, speaker

> Dum cōnspīrō spērō!

Conspiracy Theory!

What is the deep secret of <u>conspirators</u> that somehow relates them to, of all things, <u>inspiration</u>? It's... <u>breathing</u>!
<u>conspirator</u> << ***con-*** (together) + ***spīrāre, spīrātum*** (to breathe)
Conspirators whisper stuff to each other, breathing loudly into each other's ears.
<u>inspiration</u> << ***in-*** (in/on) + ***spīrāre, spīrātum*** (to breathe)
Inspiration breathes a spirit of creativity into a person's heart.
To <u>expire</u> (= to die, to end) is to 'breathe out' your last breath.
To <u>perspire</u> (= to sweat) is to 'breathe through' the pores of your skin.

Under a Yoke

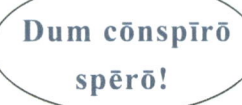

<u>subjugate</u> (= to defeat) <<< Inside <u>subjugate</u> there is a <u>yoke</u>!
jugum (yoke) joined the necks of oxen so that they pulled a cart or a plow together. When ancient Romans won a war, they made an arch from two spears and put a yoke on top. Then they made the leaders of the defeated tribe pass under that arch as a symbol of bowing down to Roman power. That custom was known as walking ***sub jugum*** – under the yoke.
sub jugum >> <u>subjugate</u> • ***jugum*** << ***jungere, jūnctum*** = to join, to connect

The Past Participle stem of the verb *jungere* gave us a bunch of English words: junction, conjunction, adjunct, conjunctivitis

LATIN PREPOSITIONS

Latin prepositions require the use of a particular case.
Prepositions *a/ab* (from, by), *ē, ex* (out of), *sine* (without),
cum (with), *de* (from), *pro* (for) – all these require the Ablative case.

fōns

quid pro quō – this for that (about people exchanging favors)
quō – Ablative case of *quid* = that
ab initiō – from the beginning • *initiō* is the Abl. case form of *initium, initiī,* n. = beginning
A fonte pūrō pūra defluit aqua. – From a clear spring clear water flows (a Roman proverb).
fōns, fontis, m. – spring, fountain • *pūrus* – clear • *ā fonte pūrō* – Abl. case of *fōns pūrus*
A fronte praecipitium, a tergō lupus. – In front, a precipice, behind, a wolf
(a Roman saying referring to a difficult situation). • *frons, frontis,* f. – front
tergum, tergī, n. – back • *ā fronte, ā tergō* – Ablative case
A tē stō. – I stand by you (I am on your side). • *tē* is Ablative case of *tu* = you (singular)
Ex nihilō nihil fit. – Out of nothing comes nothing. (You can't make something out of nothing.)
Ex nihilō is the Ablative case of **nihil** n. = nothing
Ex minimo crescit,
Sed non cito fama quiescit.
Rumor grows from a smallest thing,
but doesn't easily [quickly] fall silent.
minimō = Ablative case of
minimum n. = the smallest
(superlative degree of *parvus*)
crēscere, crētum = to grow
cito = fast (adverb)
quiēscere, quiētum = to fall silent, to rest
E veritate odium. – From truth [comes] hatred.
(Some people can't handle the truth.)
vēritāte = Ablative case of • *vēritās, vēritātis,* f. = truth • *odium, odiī,* n. = hatred << odious

deus ex māchinā = a god from a machine
(help that nobody expected)
māchinā = Ablative case of
māchina, māchinae, f. = machine
Deus ex māchinā is a reference to a crane
that brought on stage actors who played
Greek gods in Greek theater. A god
always appeared at the last moment
to help the heroes and punish the evildoers.

Artem natura superat, sine vī, sine cūrā. –

Nature surpasses (beats) art, without effort, without care/thought.

artem = Accusative case of **ars, artis,** f. • **vī** = Ablative case of **vīs, vīs,** f. = force, effort

cūrā = Ablative case of • **cūra, cūrae,** f. = care, trouble

superāre, superātum = to surpass, to overcome

cum grānō salis = with a grain of salt

(to accept a statement with doubt)

grānō = Ablative case of **grānum, grānī,** n. = grain

salis = Genitive case of **sāl, salis,** m. = salt

de pīlō pendet – it hangs by a hair

pīlō = Ablative case of • **pīlus, pīlī,** m. = hair

pendere, pēnsum = to hand, to weigh << expensive, pensive, pension, pendant, pendulum

The Latin phrase *sine cūrā* produced the English sinecure – a position or office that requires little or no work but provides a nice salary.

Prepositions **ad** (to, near), **ante** (before), **post** (after) and **ad** (to, toward) are used with the Accusative case.

ante merīdiem – abbreviated to A.M. – before noon

post merīdiem – abbreviated to P.M. – after noon

merīdiem – Accusative case of **merīdiēs** = noon

nihil ad me – 'nothing to me,' 'nothing in comparison with me'

me – Accusative case of **ego** = I

Ante victōriam ne canas triumphum. – Don't sing triumph (triumphal songs) before the victory.

victōriam = Accusative case of **victōria, victōriae,** f.

triumphum = Accusative case of **triumphus, triumphī,** m.

post bellum auxilium – help after the war (help that arrives too late)

bellum = Accusative case of **bellum** n. = war

argūmentum ad hominem – 'the argument to the man' – a legal term describing an attempt to threaten or coerce a person

hominem – Accusative case of **homō, hominis,** m. = man, human

The Latin expression **ad īnfīnītum** means 'to infinity,' 'going on forever.'

ad finem = to the end

ad nauseam is 'to the point of nausea' – said about something that keeps repeating to the point of boredom

Quid ad Mercurium? – What in the world? What for Mercury's sake?
('What does this have to do with the matter?') • *Mercurium* – Accusative case of *Mercurius*

Prepositions *in* (inside) and *sub* (under) are used with the Ablative case if you indicate location, but with the Accusative case if you indicate direction of movement – 'into'.

sub rosā –
said in secret, not to be repeated
rosā – Ablative case of *rosa* = a rose
The rose was the flower dedicated to Harpocrates, the god of silence. In the Roman world, if the host of a meeting or a party had a rose hanging over his seat, the participants knew that nothing said at that event should be shared with anyone.

Falsum in ūnō, falsum in omnī. –
Untrustworthy in one thing,
untrustworthy in everything.
falsum n. = false, untrustworthy << false
<< *fallere, falsum* = to cheat
ūnō = Ablative case of *ūnus* = one
In triviō sum. – I am at the crossroads (I have to take a difficult decision).
triviō = Ablative case of *trivium, triviī*, n. = a place where three roads meet
de fūmō in flammam – from smoke to flame ('out of the frying pan into the fire')
fūmō = Ablative case of *fūmus, fūmī*, m. = smoke
flammam = Accusative case of *flamma, flammae*, f. = flame
Ex umbrā in sōlem – 'from the shade into the light' –
is a Latin phrase used to say 'something that was unclear has been explained.'
ex umbrā is the Ablative case of *umbra* = shade
in solem is the Accusative case of *sōl* = sun

umbrāculum

False Friends?

Is there anything in common between inside and coincide?
Nothing in common between these two!
inside = in + side • coincide << *co-* (together) + *in-* + *cadere, cāsum* (to fall)
A coincidence is when events, by chance, happen to fall on the same date.
The closest relative of coincide is the word case formed from *cāsum* – the Past Participle of *cadere* (to fall). So, when spelling coincide, remember there is a case in it – go for *C*!

possess and obsess, on the other hand, have something in common – sitting!
possess << *potis* (owner) + *sedēre, sessum* (to sit)
obsess << *obsīdere, obsessum* – to blockade, besiege << *ob-* (against) + *sedēre, sessum* (to sit)
Just remember, possess possesses more *S*'s than obsess!

Vehicle? Really?

Why does vehicle have such a crazy spelling? It's because vehicle comes from the Latin
vehere, vectum – to carry
The Past Participle of this verb – *vectum* – gave us vector. Isn't that interesting?

Latin Pronouns

Time to learn Latin personal pronouns!
I – *ego* << egotistic, ecocentric, ego • you – *tu* • he – *is* • she – *ea* • it – *id*
we – *nos* • you (plural) – *vos* • they (male) – *ei* • they (female) – *eae* • they (neuter) – *ea*
se – self

Equus vehit puellam.

id est – abbreviated to *i.e.* – 'that is'

Latin pronouns change case forms – **decline** – like nouns.

	SINGULAR			PLURAL		
	m	f	n	m	f	n
Nom.	*is*	*ea*	*id*	*eī / iī*	*eae*	*ea*
Gen.	*eius*	*eius*	*eius*	*eōrum*	*eārum*	*eōrum*
Dat.	*eī*	*eī*	*eī*	*eīs / iīs*	*eīs / iīs*	*eīs / iīs*
Acc.	*eum*	*eam*	*id*	*eōs*	*eās*	*ea*
Abl.	*eō*	*eā*	*eō*	*eīs / iīs*	*eīs / iīs*	*eīs / iīs*

Dative case: • *dā mihī* – give me / to me • *dā nōbīs* – give us / to us
Accusative case: • *vocat mē* – he/she calls me • *vocat vōs* – he/she calls you (plural)

Quae suprā nōs, nihil ad nōs. – What's above us, is nothing to us.
(Things way beyond our reach are not worth our effort. 'What is too high, let it fly.')
nōs is Accusative case required by the prepositions *suprā* and *ad.*
Qui amat mē, amat et canem meum. – He who loves me, loves my dog too.
mē – Accusative case of *ego* • *canem meum* – Accusative case of *canis meus* = my dog

The Roman name of the Mediterranean Sea was **Mare Nostrum** – 'our sea.'
Mediterranean << *medium* (middle) + *terra* (land)

se (self, on your own, apart) = appears as a prefix in many Latin and English words:
security << *se-* + *cura* (care)
secret << *se-* + *cernere* (to separate, to distinguish)
secretary comes from the Medieval Latin *secretarius* – an assistant, one who knows your secrets
select << *se-* + *legere* (to gather, to read)
secede << *se-* + *cēdere* (to go)
separate << *se-* + *parāre* (o prepare)
per se – by itself • E.g.: This fact *per se* is important. – This fact 'by itself' is important.

THE MULTI-SIDED THINGS

ambi- is a Latin prefix that carries the meaning of 'both sides, multi-sided.'
It comes from the verb *ambīre, ambītum* – to go around. So what are the 'sides' in
ambivalent, ambidextrous, ambiguous?

No sin in sensation!
<< **sēnsus** (feeling, sensation)

ambiguous << *ambi-* + *agere* (to do, to act)
Ambiguous means 'open to more than one interpretation,' unclear in its meaning.
ambiguous statement = a potentially misleading statement
ambivalent << *ambi* + *valēns* (healthy)
Ambivalent means 'having mixed feelings or contradictory ideas about something or someone.'
An 'ambivalent attitude' is undecided, sending a mixed message.
ambidextrous << *ambi-* + *dextera* (right hand)
An ambidextrous person is 'right-handed on both sides,' or, in other words, someone
whose both hands are equally dominant. Dexterity is skill in performing various tasks,
especially when working with one's hands.

The adjective ambient means 'surrounding, appearing all around.'
ambient << *ambiēns* (Present Participle)
<< *ambīre* = to go around << *ambi-* (around) + *īre* (to go)

Ambīre pops up in some unexpected places. How about ambitious?
What does ambition have to do with going around? A lot!
Imagine a Roman political candidate (*candidātus Rōmānus*) wearing his
white toga (*toga candida*) *going around* (*ambiēns*) asking for votes:
Who can be more ambitious than him?

SUFFIXES -TURE, -ABLE, -IBLE

Many English words of Latin origin contain the suffix -ture. Latin: *structūra* – English: structure
In Latin, the *-ūra* suffix is attached to Past Participles of verbs in order to turn them into nouns.
Because many Past Participles have *T* in their stem, the resulting nouns have the *-tura* ending.
struere, strūctum – to build • *strūctum* + *- ūra* = *structūra* – building >> structure
venīre, ventum – to come >> venture, adventure
colere, cultum – to cultivate >> *cultūra* >> culture, agriculture   **frāctūra**
partīre, partītum – to share, to divide >> departure
nāscī, nātum – to be born >> *nātūra* >> nature
Nātūra artis magistra. – Nature is the teacher of the arts.
capere, captum – to capture >> *captūra* >> capture   **Patella frācta est.**
facere, factum – to do >> manufacture
pōnere, positum – to put, to place >> *positūra* – position, situation >> posture
sīgnāre, sīgnātum – to mark >> signature
temperāre, temperātum – to temper, to moderate >> *temperātūra* = measure >> temperature
frangere, frāctum – to break >> *fractūra* – breach >> fracture
sculpere, sculptum – to carve >> *sculptūra* >> sculpture
miscēre, mixtum – to mix >> *mixtūra* >> mixture
Also: architecture, caricature, conjecture, pasture, future, portraiture, aperture, creature, feature, fixture, lecture, overture, puncture, torture...

pictūra   sculptūra   cultūra

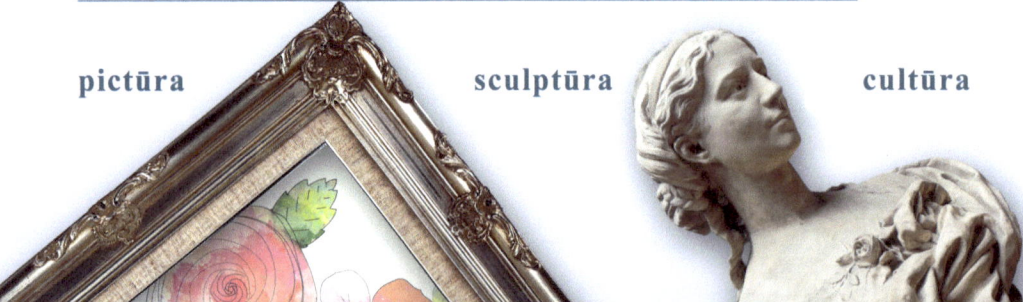

Most English words with the 'cher' sound are of Latin origin and are spelled with **-ture** – structure, adventure, aperture. The spelling 'cher' only appears with words ending with **-ch** – teach – teacher, catch – catcher, snatch – snatcher.

Two very common English suffixes **-able** and **-ible** come from the Latin suffix **-bilis**. In Latin, this suffix turned verbs into adjectives. Whether it was **-able** or **-ible** depended on whether the stem of the verb ended in **-a** (**ama-re** = to love), **-e** (**crede-re** = to believe), or **-i** (**audi-re** = to hear).

However, in English
-ible appears mainly in words of obvious Latin origin, after roots that cannot stand alone – visible, possible
-able attaches itself to non-Latin roots (and sometimes to Latin roots) to create new words that never existed in Latin. These roots are often found in English as stand-alone words – depend – dependable, wash – washable, do – doable

Examples:
-ible in words that came from Latin adjectives:
crēdere – to believe >> *crēdibilis* >> credible
vincere – to conquer >> *vincibilis* >> invincible, convincible
dūcere, ductum – to lead >> *ducibilis* – easy to lead >> deducible, reducible
posse – to be able to, can >> *possibilis* >> possible
flectere, flexum – to bend >> *flexibilis* >> flexible
legere, lēctum – to read >> *legibilis* – easy to read >> legible, intelligible, negligible

No rant in apparently!
<< *appārēns* (appearing)

-able in words of non-Latin origin:
lovable, likable, drinkable, readable
-able in words that use Latin roots to create words that didn't exist in Latin:
movēre – to move >> movable
ūtī, ūsum – to use >> usable

No up in surprise!
<< *sur* (over) + *prēndere* (to catch, to understand)

Is Admiral to be Admired?

No! Admiral comes from Arabic *amiral* ('leader' – same root as *emir* = prince). But English grammarians presumed that it came from the Latin verb *admīrārī, admīrātum* (to admire), and that in Latin it had the prefix *ad-*. So they stuck a *D* inside admiral!

Emigrant, Immigrant, and Migrant

Is one of these a misspell? What is the difference between emigrant and immigrant? Let's take a look at the origin of these words.

emigrate << *ex-* (out of) + **migrāre** (to move, to leave)
immigrate << *in-* (into, inside) + **migrāre** (to move, to leave)
So the difference between these words comes down to
the difference between *ex-* (out) and *in-* (into).
An emigrant is someone who leaves a country – moves out of a country.
An immigrant is a person who moves into a country.
So it can be the same person, but in relation to his old country he is an emigrant, while in relation to his new country he is an immigrant.
There is also a migrant – a person who moves from one place to another. Maybe it's a new country, or maybe not.

Some words have a positive or negative
connotation – an additional flavor of either approval or disapproval.
connotation << **con-** (with, together) + *notāre, notātum* (to record, to mean)
Emigrant and immigrant have neither a positive nor negative connotation. But the word migrant often carries negative connotations. It's often a person who violates the law by moving into a country without permission, and therefore is perceived as a dangerous, unwelcome arrival.

Locus meus est!

All Those Places

locus, locī, m. = place • *locāre, locātum* = to place, to locate
All the words below have **locus / locāre** in them, and therefore are spelled with *O*:
locate, dislocate, locator, location, local, locality, locomotive, locomotion

Suffixes -al and -ar

The suffixes **-al, -ar** are usually unstressed in English words. They are not pronounced clearly, which could cause misspells – unless you know the original Latin words with these suffixes. As you do!

The English suffix **-al** comes from the Latin suffix **–alis.**

original << *orīginālis* << *orīgo, orīginis,* f. – beginning

equal << *aequālis* (equal) << *aequus* – even, flat

equinox – *aequus + nox* (night) • Equinox occurs twice each year when day and night are of equal length (always around the 22nd of September and 20th of March).

social << *sociālis* << *socius* = partner • brutal << *brūtālis* << *brūtus* = stupid, cruel

personal << *persōnālis* << *persōna* = mask • animal << *animālis* << *anima* = soul

territorial << *territōrium* (territory) << *terra* • cerebral << *cerebrum* (brain)

A variation of **-al** is **-ar**, coming from Latin **-aris/-arius**.

similar << *similāris* << *simile* = comparison • popular << *populāris* << *populus* = people

military << *mīlitāris* << *mīles* = soldier • honorary << *honōrārius* << *honor* = honor

vulgar << *vulgaris* << *vulgus* (common people, crowd)

linear << *līneāre* = to line up << *līnea* = a string • familiar << *familiāris* << *familia* = family

momentary << *mōmentarius* = brief << *mōmentum* = moment

voluntary << *voluntārius* << *voluntās* = free will

notary << *notārius* = clerk << *notāre* (to record)

secular << *sēculāris* (of a century) << *saeculum* (century, age)

> No stance in existence!
> *existēns* (existing)
> << *ex* (out of) +
> *sistēre* (to stop)

What's Inside?

Inside prejudice there sits a judge! Prejudice happens when people pre-judge one another, forming opinions that are not based on actual evidence. All the words below come from the Latin *jūdex, jūdicis,* m. = judge, and retain the *jud* in their spelling:

judge, judicial, prejudice, judiciary, adjudicate

Perpendicular has a pendulum in it! Actually, not a pendulum, but a 'plumb line' –
a string with a weight at the end used to determine verticality or depth.

perpendiculum = a plumb line

The root *pend* found in many English words comes from the Latin
pendere, pēnsum = to hang, to weigh, to pay out
>> expend, suspend, expense, suspense, compensate, append, pendant, appendix
The often-misspelled words from this group – perpendicular and compensate –
both have kept the ***pend / pens*** root.

Design has a signature in it – ***signum, signī***, n. = mark, signature, emblem
sign, design, resign, consign, signature, designation

Inside comprehend / comprehension and apprehend / apprehension hides
prehendere, prehēnsum = to grasp
To comprehend means to grasp an idea; to apprehend means to grasp either an idea
or a person! Both verbs have retained the *E*'s of ***prehendere.***

There is precious inside appreciate! • precious, appreciate, depreciate << ***pretium*** (value)

What is inside result and insult? You will be surprised!
Why are these two words so suspiciously similar??
result << *re-* (back) + ***saltāre, saltātum*** (to jump)
insult << *in-* (on/in) + ***saltāre, saltātum*** (to jump)   Amō saltāre!
That's right: result and insult share a 'jump'!
The result is something that 'jumps' back at the person who performs an action.
An insult is when someone 'jumps' at you with a rude comment.

HOUSES AND PALACES

urbs, urbis, f. – city • ***domus*** f. – house >> domestic • ***palātium, palātiī,*** n. – palace >> palatial
vīlla, vīllae, f. – country house, villa • ***īnsula, īnsulae,*** f. – island, apartment building
ārea, āreae, f. – open space, area around a house • ***forum, forī,*** n. – square
via, viae, f. – road, street • ***via media*** – middle road
porta, portae, f. – gate • ***cubiculum, cubiculī,*** n. – room >> cubicle
hortus, hortī, m. – garden >> horticulture • ***focus, focī,*** m. – fireplace, focus
ātrium, ātriī, n. – welcoming room in a Roman villa, reception hall >> atrium
mūrus, mūrī, m. – wall >> mural, intramural

Domus mea parva est.

Please answer questions using the nouns listed on the previous page, the verb *esse*, and a few of these adjectives and pronouns:

māgnus/māgna/māgnum – large

ēnormis, ēnormis, ēnorme – huge, enormous • *parvus/parva/parvum* – small

minisculus, miniscula, minisculum – very small

meus / mea / meum – my, mine • *tuus / tua / tuum* – your, yours

mihī – to me; *est mihī* – I have • *tibī* – to you; *estne tibī...?* – do you have...?

Est domus tua māgna aut (or) *parva?* • *Est cubiculum tuum māgnum aut parvum?*
Est via tua māgna aut parva? • *Est urbs tua māgna aut parva?*
Estne tibī hortus? • *Estne tibī focus?* • *Estne tibī palātium?*

No Playdates with Them!

lūdere, lūsum means 'to play' But be warned: Some kids don't play fair, and look what happens:

de- (down, undo) + *ludere* (to play) >>> *dēlūdere* = to deceive >>> delusion

in- (at) + *ludere* (to play) >>> *illūdere* = to mock, to trick >>> illusion

Some other kids play between themselves and don't invite you. Here's how we call this in Latin:

con- + *ludere* (to play) >>> *collūdere* (to play together) >> collusion

They collude to exclude you!

exclude << e*x-* (out,from) + *clūdere, clūsum* (to close, to lock) – 'to lock out'

Remember: *con-* and *in-* change *N* to *L* if followed by a root starting with *L*.

But *de-* doesn't play those 'consonant gymnastics' games, and never causes double consonants.

DE- OF DOOM AND DIS- OF DIVISION

Latin prefix *de-* (down, away from, not) is easy. It ends in a vowel and never causes a doubling of consonants. However, it is typically unstressed, and that results in misspells, such as 'di-,' perhaps because it gets confused with *dis-*.

Let's take a look at some popular words with *de-* and try to remember their spelling. So many words with *de-* have negativity in their meaning, that I decided to divide the words with this prefix into 2 groups: *De-* of Doom and Okay *De-*.

De- of Doom

denigrate << *de-* + *niger* (black) – to blacken, to put down
despise, despicable << *de-* + *specere, spectum* (to look at)
destruct << *de-* + *struere, strūctum* (to build)
defame << *de-* + *fāma* (fame, reputation) – to slander
degrade << *de-* + *gradī* (to walk, to step) – treat with contempt
decline << *de-* + *clīnāre* (to incline, to bend) – to reject, to grow worse
depopulate << *de-* + *populus* (people) – to make empty
devalue << *de-* + *valere* (to be strong, healthy, to be worth) – to reduce the value
deface << *de-* + *faciēs* (appearance) – to spoil the surface of something
decease << *de-* + *cēdere* (to go) – to die
deceive << *de-* + *capere* (to take)
deflate << *de-* + *flāre, flātum* (to blow)
degenerate << *de-* + *generāre* (to produce) – to grow worse
demented << *de-* + *mēns, mentis,* f. (mind, intellect) – of people who have lost clear thinking
depose << *de-* + *pōnere, positum* (to place) – to overthrow, to remove from office

Prefix *de-* easily attaches itself to words of non-Latin origin:
debase, debunk

I am doomed!

OK *De-*

decode << *de-* + *codex* (book, law)
declare << *dēclārāre* (to announce) << *de-* + *clarus* (clear)
decide << *de-* + *caedere* (to cut) • deduce << *de-* + *dūcere* (to lead)
descend << *de-* + *scandere* (to climb) • delegate << *de-* + *lēgāre* (to send as an ambassador)

How about disease? No *de-* in disease! And no cease in disease! • disease << *dis* + ease

Prefix *dis-* (apart, away, in different directions) can't resist roots that start with *F*.
The moment it sees *F*, it turns into *dif-* • different << *dis-* + *ferre* (to carry)
If you take the word disease << *dis* + ease
and replace ease / easy with the Latin *facilis* (easy to do), you get
difficult << *dis-* + *facilis* = not easy
Wouldn't English spelling be easier if, instead of difficult and different, we had
'disfacilis' and 'disferrent'? Hmmm... Actually, maybe not.

Whenever you see *diss*, it's usually a result of *dis-* + roots starting with *S*.
dissent << *dis-* + *sentire* (feel, think) • dissuade << *dis-* + *suādēre, suāsum* (to advise)
dissatisfy << *dis-* + *satis* (enough) + *facere* (to do, to make)

QUALITIES OF A PERSON

fēlīx – m., f., n. – happy • *felicitās, felicitātis,* f. – happiness
ānxius, ānxia, ānxium – anxious • *anxietas* – anxiety
ambitio – ambition • *ambitiōsus, ambitiōsa, ambitiōsum* – ambitious
iratus, irata – angry >> *ira* – anger >> irate
malus, mala – evil
arrogāns – arogant • *arrogantia, arrogantiae,* f. – arrogance
audacia – bravery • *audāx* – m., f., n. – audacious, brave
timidus, timida – fearful >> timid
invidus, invida – envious, jealous • *invidia* – jealousy, envy
laetus, laeta – joyful • *miser, misera* – miserable • *trīstis* m., f. – sad
sōlus, sōla – lonely • *urbanus, urbana* – civilized, polite • *crudelis* m., f. – cruel >> crude
fraudulentus – deceitful, dishonest • *fraus, fraudis* – fraud >> fraudulent
fidēlis m., f. – loyal, faithful << *fidēs, fideī,* f. – faith
dīligēns m., f. – diligent, careful • *īgnōrāns* m., f. – ignorant • *sapiēns* m., f. – wise
honorabilis – honorable
iniūstus, iniūsta – unjust >> injustice
intellegēns m., f. – intelligent

miser   laetus

timidus

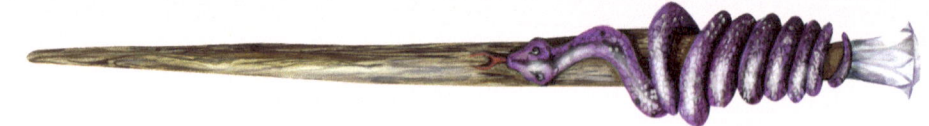
baculum magicum

Use the verb *esse* (*est*) and the adjectives from the previous page to describe the following fairy tale characters:

Snow White = *Albanix* << **alba** = white + **nix** = snow
Cinderella = *Cinerella* << **cinis, cineris,** m. = ash
Lupus – the Wolf in *Little Red Riding Hood*
Imperātor – the emperor in *The Emperor's New Clothes* by Hans Christian Andersen
Rēgīna Mala – the Evil Queen in *Snow White*
Rēgis Fīlius (Son of the King) – Prince Charming in *Cinderella*
Noverca – stepmother – Cinderella's evil stepmother
Aladdin
Bēstia – the Beast in *Beauty and the Beast*
sorōrēs Cinerellae – Cinderella's sisters

candēla   penna

liber magicus

Drowning in Homophones!

Help!!! I'm drowning in homophones (words that sound the same)!!! Latin to the rescue!

dissent | descent
dissent – to disagree, to think differently << ***dis-*** (differently) + ***sentire*** (to feel, think)
descent – to come down << ***de-*** (down) + ***scandere*** (to climb)
The *SC* of scandere also appears in ascend, transcend, condescend

accept | except
accept – receive << ***accipere*** = receive, get without effort << ***ad-*** (toward) + ***capere*** (to take)
except – excluding << ***ex-*** (out) + ***capere*** (to take)

vocation | vacation
vocation – a strong feeling that you are good at a particular profession
<< ***vocātiō*** (a calling) << ***vocāre, vocātum*** = to call >> vocal, invoke, revoke
vacation – holidays, time off school << ***vacātiō*** (freedom, immunity)
<< ***vacāre, vacātum*** = to be free, empty >> vacuum

addition | edition
addition << ***ad-*** (toward) + ***dare, datum*** (to give)
edition << ***ēdere, ēditum*** = to put forward, to make known

lucerna magica

tapētum magicum

council | counsel

council (a group of people meeting to work something out) << *concilium* (public gathering)

counsel (advisor) << *cōnsilium* = plan, advice

vain | vein

vain = having an exaggerated opinion of oneself; also in vain = without success or result << *vānus* = empty, useless

vein = blood vessel << *vēna* = a blood vessel

veil | vale

veil = fabric face or head covering << *vēlāre, vēlātum* = to cover << *vēlum* = a sail, cloth

vale = valley << *vallis* = valley

air | heir

air (contents of the atmosphere) << *āēr* = air

heir (a person who inherits something) << *hērēs* = heir, heiress

cereal | serial

cereal (grain) << *Ceres* (Roman goddess of agriculture)

serial (in a series, in a row) << *seriēs* (row, chain) << *serere* = to join

vēlum

Totally Hopeless Homophone Cases

These word pairs below... Even our mighty Latin can hardly help us here! Seriously, people: I give up. ... Oh, ok... maybe not yet!

flōrēs

compliment (a flattering comment) **| complement** (an additional feature)

Both words come from *complēre, complētum* – to fill up << *con-* (together) + p*lere* (to fill). Compliment came to English via Italian – that's why these two words ended up with different spellings. How to remember their correct spelling?

One way is to remember that complement, complete, and plenty come from the same root – they carry the same idea of 'filling, completing.'

Here is how I remember the correct spelling of compliment: compliment has an *I* in it – and *I* love compliments!

pōculum plēnum

flour | flower

This is another hopeless case, because both have the same origin:

flour and flower << *flōs, flōris,* m. = flower

Flour was made from the best portions of grains – maybe that's why they called it 'flower.' Flour was actually spelled 'flower' until the 19th century, when it was decided to change the spelling in order to stop the confusion. Just remember: There are NO flowers in flour!

principle | principal

Can one be an unprincipled principal, or principal who is principally an individual without any principles as a matter of principle? Yes, I guess. But if you happen to study at that principal's school – run! Use that centrifugal force that Newton described in his *Principia* (The Principles). Jokes aside, what's going on with these two nouns?
Both come from *prīnceps* = a leader
principal << *principālis* (first, most important) << *prīnceps* = a leader
<< *primus* (first) + *capere* (to take)
principle << *prīncipium* (beginning) << *prīnceps* = a leader
Here is how to remember the spelling... There is a pal in the principal –
that's if your school principal happens to be a nice highly-principled one, of course.

Carry On!

The Latin verb *ferre* means 'to carry / to bring.' Some Latin prefixes, champions of 'consonant gymnastics,' are eager to be friends with *ferre* and swap their consonants for *F*.
differ << *dis-* (apart, divide) + *ferre* • suffer << *sub-* (under, after) + *ferre*
Other suffixes keep their identity.
The words below are easy to spell as long as you remember the spelling of *ferre* >> fer
defer << *de-* (down, from) + *ferre* (to carry) – to put off
transfer << *trans-* (across) + *ferre* (to carry) • refer << *re-* (again, back) + *ferre* (to carry)
prefer << *pre-* (before, in front) + *ferre* (to carry)
confer << *con-* (together) + *ferre* (to carry) – to grant, to give
infer << *in-* (inside) + *ferre* (to carry) – to conclude
In the words below *fer* is unstressed, so it helps to know the root here to avoid misspells.
circumference << *circum* (around) + *ferre* (to carry)
coniferous << *cōnus* (cne) + *ferre* (to carry) – 'cone carrying' – pine trees and fir trees
vociferous << *vōx* (voice) + *ferre* (to carry) – 'voice carrying' – loud people with a lot of opinions
aquifer << *aqua* (water) + *ferre* (to carry) – 'water carrying' – an underground water-rich layer

Prefix In-

Prefix *in-* is one of the champions of 'consonant gymnastics.' See what it can do!

in- >> *il-*

illuminate << *in-* + *lūmināre, lūminātum* (to illuminate) • illegal << *in-* + *lēx, lēgis,* f. (law)
illustrate << *in-* + *lūstrāre, lūstrātum* (to illuminate) • illusion << *in-* + *lūdere, lūsum* (to play)
illiterate << *in-* + *lītera, līterae,* f. (letter of the alphabet)

in- >> *ir-*

irregular << *in-* + *rēgulāre, rēgulātum* (to direct) • irrational << *in-* + *ratiō, ratiōnis,* f. (reason)
irrigate << **in-** + **rigāre, rigātum** (to water)

in- >> *im-*

immigrant << *in-* + *migrāre, migrātum* (migrate) • immobile << *in-* + *mōbilis* (movable)
immunity << *in-* + *mūnīre, mūnītum* (to build, to protect)
immortal << *in-* + *mors, mortis,* f. (death) • immature << *in-* + *mātūrus* (ripe)
immense << *in-* + *mētīrī, mēnsum* (to measure)

Gerundive

Latin Gerundive is an adjective derived from the passive future tense forms of verbs.
It usually carries the meaning of 'something that has to be done / must be done in the future.'
The endings of the Gerundive are *-ndus* (m.), *-nda* (f.), *-ndum* (n.)
Many English words came from Latin gerundives:
agenda is plural of *agendus* = something that has to be done << *agere, āctum* = to do
propaganda is plural of *prōpāgandus* = something that must be increased, propagated
<< *prōpāgāre, prōpāgātum* = to propagate, to grow
memorandum – neuter Gerundive, something that has to be remembered
<< *memorāre, memorātum* = to remember
legend << *legendus,* Gerundive of *legere* = to read, to gather
conundrum (a mystery, a riddle) << *cōnandum* (an action to be attempted) neuter Gerundive
of *cōnārī, cōnātum* = to try, to attempt

Popular Latin expressions *modus operandi* (a method of doing something) and
modus vivendi (way of life) contain Genitive case gerundives:
operandī << *operandus* = should be done/performed << *operārī, operātum* = to work
vivendī << *vīvendus* = should be lived << *vīvere, vīctum* = to live

Many names that have **ND** come from gerundives;

<u>Amanda</u> – one that should be loved << ***amāre, amātum*** = to love

<u>Miranda</u> – one that should be admired << ***mīrārī, mīrātum*** = to admire

Mīrandus sum!

equus marīnus

De gustibus nōn disputandum. – Matters of taste should not be disputed.

de gustibus = 'about tastes'

disputandum = neuter Gerundive << ***disputāre, disputātum*** = to argue

Arrogantia nōn ferenda. – Arrogance should not be tolerated.

ferenda is a Gerundive of the verb ***ferre, lātum*** = to carry, to bear

Religio docenda, nōn coercenda. – Religion must be taught, not forced.

docenda – Gerundive of ***docēre, doctum*** = to teach >> <u>doctor, doctrine</u>

coercenda – Gerundive of ***coercēre, coercitum*** = to limit, to repress >> to <u>coerce, coercion</u>

Math terminology is full of Gerundive forms:

<u>dividend</u> (a number to be divided by another number) << ***dīvidendum*** = thing to be divided << ***dīvidere, dīvīsum*** – to divide

<u>addend</u> (a number which is added to another) << ***addendus*** = thing to be added << ***addere, additum*** – to add

<u>minuend</u> (a number from which another is to be subtracted) << ***minuendum*** – thing from which something is to be subtracted << ***minuere*** – subtract

<u>subtrahend</u> (a number to be subtracted) << ***subtrahendus*** = to be subtracted << ***subtrahere, subtractum*** – to take away << ***trahere, tractum*** – to pull, to draw

<u>multiplicand</u> (a number to be multiplied) << ***multiplicandum*** = to be multiplied << ***multiplicāre multiplicātum*** – to multiply

quod erat demonstrandum, abbreviated to **QED**, means 'what had to be shown/proved.' It is added at the end of a logical or mathematical proof to indicate that the task of proving is complete.

Dīvide et impera.
Divide and rule.

Carthago dēlenda est. – Carthage must be destroyed.
This phrase was made popular by Cato the Censor,
a politician of the Roman Republic, prior to the
Third Punic War (149–146 BC) between Rome and Carthage.
dēlenda is the Gerundive form of
dēlēre, dēlētum – to destroy, to <u>delete</u>

<u>minute</u>
<< ***minuta*** =
a small portion or piece
<< ***minuere, minūtum*** –
to subtract, to reduce

All the 'Other' Things

Aliēnus? Aliēna?

Aliēnum sum.

Latin pronoun *alius* (m) / *alia* (f) / *aiud* (n) means 'another'; pronoun *alter* (m) / *altera* (f) / *alterum* (n) means 'the other.' These two pronouns appear in a few English words of Latin origin:

alias – another name << *aliās* (at another time) << *alius* (another)

alien << *aliēnus* (unfamiliar, unfriendly, a stranger)

alibi – evidence that a person was not at the scene of a crime when that crime was committed << *alibi* (somewhere else)

alter appears in <u>alter, alternate, alternative, altercation, alt</u> (computer key), <u>altruist</u> (a person who cares about the well-being of others), <u>altruistic</u>

alter ego – "another I" – a person's pseudonym (fictitious name) or a friend who acts on one's behalf

Alter ipse amicus. – A friend is another self.

patella volāns

The Longest-Possible Word Generator

Drum roll, please! Ladies and Gentlemen, please put your hands together for my famous **The Longest-Possible Word Generator**! With this novel system of rare ingenuity you can beat university professors in coming up with extremely long and mostly meaningless words! Just combine any of these prefixes, suffixes, roots, and endings in any numbers and configurations, and enjoy! Your parents and friends will be impressed!

But first, for inspiration, here are some actual, real words from the vocabulary of lawyers, politicians and university professors:

antidisestablishmentarianism • extraconstitutionality • incomprehensibility

And here – for more inspiration – is a list of words I have just generated. Possible meanings are provided!

antipredispensatory – anti-pre-dis-pens-atory
(being against distributing something before it is approved for distribution)
E.g.: Let's take an antipredispensatory attitude to giving candy before trick-or-treating.

ultradesubreductionism – ultra-de-sub-re-duct-ionism
(an extreme case of reversing the act of reducing something below its accepted lower limit)
E.g.: Because of my grandma's ultradesubreductionist position on weeds, her garden is overgrown with dandelions.

proconferdictory – pro-con-fer-dict-ory (actively involved in getting the word out to the community)
E.g.: I received a proconferdictory message inviting me to our neighborhood block party.

maleducule – male-duc-cule (an evil leader who is very small)
E.g.: Who is this maleducule? – It's our class bully.

omnidisinaugmentation – omni-dis-in-aug-ment-ation
(when everything stops growing inside itself)
E.g.: My latest batch of slime has fallen into a state of omnidisinaugmentation.

sublunolauding – sub-luno-laud-ing (praising whatever is under the moon)
E.g.: This guy is a truly sublunolausive character. He was sublunolauding like a maniac at our Christmas party.

And now... mix, match, and impress!

Prefixes	Roots		Suffixes, endings, connecting vowels
bene-	*aqua* (water)	*reducti* (reduce)	*-cule (tiny)*
male-	*fer* (carry)	*augment* (increase)	*-issimus (superlative degree)*
pre-	*dict* (say)	*fix* (fix)	*-able* (capable)
pro-	*duc* (lead)	*mix* (mix)	*-a-*
con-	*hab* (have)	*lud/lus* (play)	*-i-*
ultra-	*jur* (law)	*astr* (star)	*-e-*
extra	*port* (carry)	*lun* (moon)	*-ology / -logy*
infra-	*scrib* (write)	*laud* (praise)	*-scent*
intra-	*sens* (feel)		*-ility / -sibility*
re-	*pens* (think)		*-nality*
in-	*terre* (earth)		*-ous / -ious / eous*
de-	*vide* (see)		*-ianism / -tism*
anti-	*pend* (hang)		*-tion / -sion*
mis-	*separa* (separation)		*-ive*
dis-	*ratio* (reason)		*-ment*
omni-	*audi* (hear)		*-estrial*
			-atory / -ory

www.ingramcontent.com/pod-product-compliance
Lightning Source LLC
Chambersburg PA
CBHW041432010526
44118CB00002B/58